The Conversation Series

Copyediting by Matthew Gaskins
Designed at M/M (Paris)
Typesetting by Selitsch Weig

Production by Printmanagement Plitt, Oberhausen

Published by
Verlag der Buchhandlung Walther König, Köln
Ehrenstr. 4, 50672 Cologne, Germany
Tel.: +49 221 20 59 6-53
verlag@buchhandlung-walther-koenig.de

The Deutsche Nationalbibliothek lists this publication
in the Deutsche Nationalbibliografie; detailed bibliographic
data are available in the Internet at http://dnb.d-nb.de.

Printed in Germany

Outside Europe
D.A.P./Distributed Art Publishers, Inc., New York
155 Sixth Avenue, New York, NY 10013, USA
Tel.: +1 212 627-1999; Fax: +1 212 627-9484
www.artbook.com

ISBN 978-3-86560-500-9

John Baldessari

Hans Ulrich Obrist

— The Conversation Series

18

Verlag der Buchhandlung Walther König, Köln

I — What I Had Left Out
Studio John Baldessari, Santa Monica, California
March 2, 2003

Hans Ulrich Obrist — **I'd like to start by focusing on your writing. What role does it play in your artistic practice?**

John Baldessari — For many years I kept notebooks and would write down my ideas in them. Then at a certain point I stopped. I figured I could just remember things! When I describe certain works, it's usually at someone's request. When I was showing at the Sonnabend Gallery, for instance, Ileana [Sonnabend] asked if I would write about the work to help her and her staff explain it to other people. I had always been a little reluctant to provide this kind of material, because I think that as soon as you explain a work, you take away some of its power. Ultimately, I did write something for her, because I thought it would be better than having the works misrepresented. But it didn't turn out as I had expected: they ended up giving the texts to critics and collectors as handouts, and then those got quoted in the press. At any rate, before the show at the Sonnabend Gallery, when I was doing the book by Coosje van Bruggen, I tried to get my notes organized for her.[1] But when she saw them, she said, "No, I would rather you just talk to me about the works. I don't need these notes so much." That's how I felt, too. When I did my second show in Europe, at the Van Abbemuseum for Rudi Fuchs ["John Baldessari," Eindhoven, 1981] and the Museum Folkwang for Jan Debbaut ["John Baldessari," Essen, 1981], I had also made notes, including materials I thought might be useful. I think they actually did use the notes as descriptions in their catalogue. And then there are lists, which are really just meant for me—to help me remember things.

Hans Ulrich Obrist — **Not unlike Georges Perec—he used to make lists for shopping and all other kinds of things.**

John Baldessari — Yes, it's a type of shorthand and probably wouldn't make sense to anybody but me.

Hans Ulrich Obrist — **There are also a lot of instructions; they're always in the same format, like index cards.**

John Baldessari — I think the instructions format is very closely connected with my teaching work and my art. When I'm teaching, I actually try to make my teaching like art. And my art probably has something to do

(1) Coosje van Bruggen, *John Baldessari – The Museum of Contemporary Art, Los Angeles, March 25-June 17, 1990* (New York: Rizzoli, 1990).

with making things clear—or not clear! A lot of my teaching methodology involves saying things obliquely. Rather than telling somebody to do something directly, I suggest something in a very oblique way, and sometimes the students end up thinking it's their idea. It's a much more effective method than saying do this or do that.

Hans Ulrich Obrist — **So in that sense they're not instructions to be followed.**

John Baldessari — Well, it's a little more covert, I think. The first book I did—*Ingres and Other Parables*[2]—started out with me writing these stories. It was for a show I did with Konrad Fischer ["John Baldessari: Ingres and Other Parables," Konrad Fischer, Düsseldorf, 1971]. They were also meant to be oblique instructions about how one might proceed in doing art. They were really meant as stories for students, with moral endings. Then it came out as a book.

Hans Ulrich Obrist — **It might be interesting for the textbook.**

John Baldessari — Absolutely, yes. Also, I have a real fondness for language. A lot of my early works were text-only pieces. I thought that if people don't understand painting, they should certainly be able to understand text or photographs because you get that in books and magazines and so on. Of course, that didn't work out so well. It was a real challenge for me to get texts and photographs into galleries and have them accepted as art. I think as soon as that battle was won…

(2) John Baldessari, *Ingres and Other Parables* (London: Studio International Publ., 1972).

INGRES

This is the story of a little known painting by Ingres. Its first owner took good care of it, but as things go, he eventually had to sell it. Succeeding owners were not so cautious about its welfare and did not take as good care of it as the first owner. That is, the second owner let the painting's condition slip a bit. Maybe it all began by letting it hang crookedly on the wall, not dusting it, maybe it fell to the floor a few times when somebody slammed the door too hard. Anyway the third owner received the Ingres with some scratches (not really tears), and the canvas buckled in one corner - paint fading here and there. Owners that followed had it retouched and so on, but the repairs never matched and the decline had begun. The painting looked pretty sad. But what was important was the documentation - the idea of Ingres; not the substance. And the records were always well-kept. A clear lineage, a good genealogy. It was an Ingres certainly, even though the painting by this time was not much.

The other day it was auctioned off. Time had not been kind to the Ingres. All that was left was one nail. Maybe the nail was of the original, maybe it was used in repairs, or maybe Ingres himself had used it to hang the painting. It was all of the Ingres that remained. In fact, it was believed to be the only Ingres nail ever offered in public sale.

Moral: If you have the idea in your head, the work is as good as done.

Ingres from *Ingres and Other Parables*, 1971

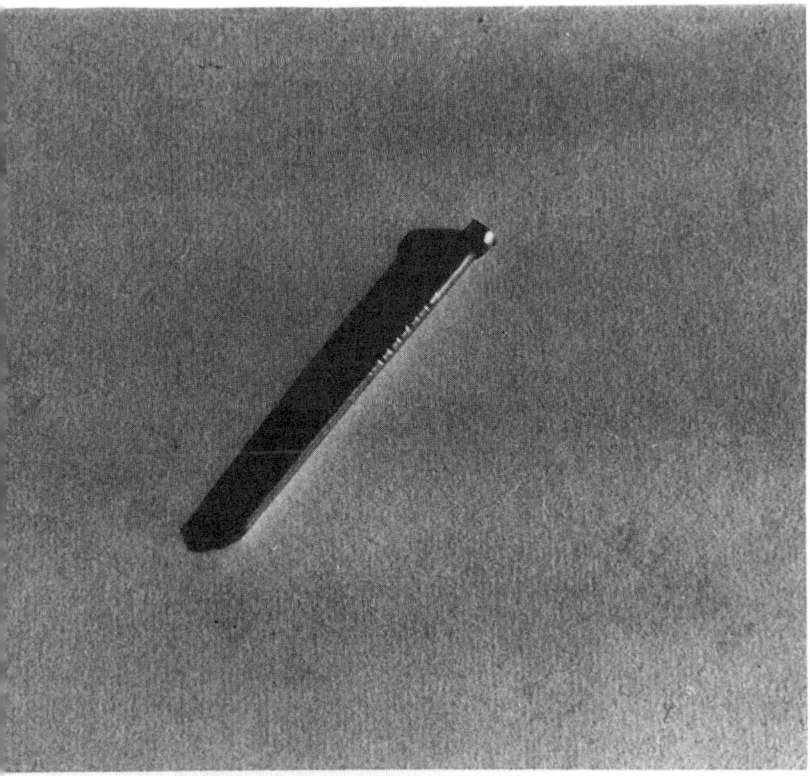

ART HISTORY

A young artist had just finished art school. He asked his instructor what he should do next. "Go to New York," the instructor replied, "and take slides of your work around to all the galleries and ask them if they will exhibit your work." Which the artist did.

He went to gallery after gallery with his slides. Each director picked up his slides one by one, held each up to the light the better to see it, and squinted his eyes as he looked. "You're too provincial an artist," they all said. "You are not in the mainstream." "We're looking for Art History."

He tried. He moved to New York. He painted tirelessly, seldom sleeping. He went to museum and gallery openings, studio parties, and artists' bars. He talked to every person having anything to do with art; travelled and thought and read constantly about art. He collapsed.

He took his slides around to galleries a second time. "Ah," the gallery directors said this time, "finally you are historical."

Moral: Historical mispronounced sounds like hysterical.

Art History from *Ingres and Other Parables*, 1971

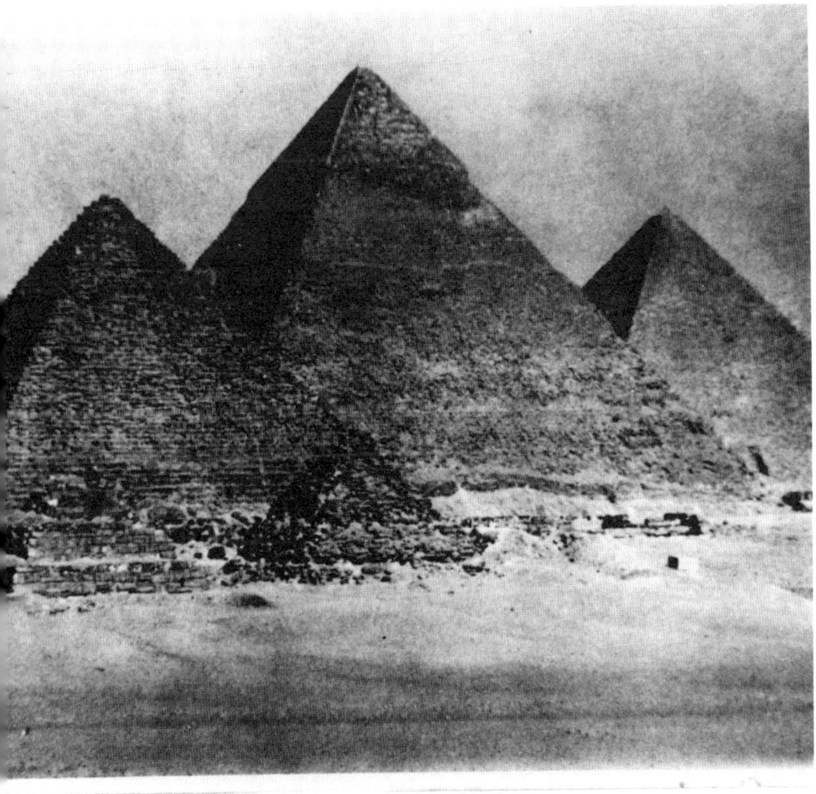

Hans Ulrich Obrist — **When would you say the battle was won?**

John Baldessari — When did we begin to see a lot of text works? Much of conceptual and minimal art of the seventies used text, and it slowly crept into the galleries. There were people, like Lawrence Weiner and [Joseph] Kosuth, who were also using text at the time. A lot of people were doing so in Europe—and, as a matter of fact, all over the world.

Hans Ulrich Obrist — **Why did the rapport between image and language play such a big role in the sixties and seventies? How do you explain that this was so important to you and to others at the time?**

John Baldessari — I think there was a considerable feeling of uneasiness about where art was going. We were into fifth- and sixth-generation abstract expressionism, and it seemed like it was exhausted. I remember the Museum of Modern Art putting on a show, trying to jumpstart a trend of "new figuration" or something like that, but that wasn't it. The lesson learned, of course, was that with art you can't predict what's going to happen. What we did was get pop art, conceptual art, and minimal art and so on. Artists were getting bored with what was going on. Conceptual and minimal artists were trying to think about art without using conventional ideas of art practice—by going outside and looking at other systems and other areas of knowledge to produce art. So using texts as information was certainly attractive.

Hans Ulrich Obrist — **What kinds of source materials were of interest to you? I recently discussed this with both Lawrence Weiner and Ed Ruscha—that is, the question of where the words and images come from in these early text pieces.**

John Baldessari — From my perspective, a word can't substitute for an image, but is equal to it. You can build with words just like you can build with imagery. Somehow I saw words and images as very abstract. The whole idea of the sliding signifier—that a word could mean anything you want it to—really fascinated me. A lot of my sources were dictionaries, things I was reading—anything I thought was enigmatic or ambiguous. I didn't want to use language in a dry way. I wanted to use it creatively.

Hans Ulrich Obrist — **I was looking back at your video works last week and it struck me how poetic and evocative the titles are. At the same time, the titles of your paintings are sometimes painted, themselves. Can you tell me about the role that titles play for you and where you draw the line between title and work?**

John Baldessari — The title of the work should be as powerful and as interesting as the work itself. To simply have a title that's less than the work is crazy. In a museum you usually have the title next to the work, and I used to want to replace them—to swap them over! That's my goal: for the title to be as powerful as the work itself. This means being as creative with the language as you are with the work. It always seems that people can dismiss words more easily than they can dismiss images, but I might be wrong. If you open a book and there's text on one side and an image on the other, you'll probably look at the image first—the images get prioritized. But I have this kind of mind that when I scan texts, certain words will stand out at me. I used to scribble them down, but now I tend to store them in my head.

Hans Ulrich Obrist — **A number of your films reveal a connection with authors; your texts also refer to writers, such as Kafka and Laurence Sterne, Sylvia Plath, and Marcel Proust. What role does literature play in your work?**

John Baldessari — I developed a habit of reading about people who were involved in creative tasks other than art. I would spend a lot of time reading about musicians and writers because they, for the most part, seem to have the same kinds of problems as artists. Being able to look at what artists do through another person's activities is a way to think more clearly about the problems we face. Or to put it another way: the last animal to criticize salt water would be a shark—if you're immersed in it, you don't see it, but if you can get into some other area, you can see things more clearly.

Hans Ulrich Obrist — **At one point you even illustrated *Tristram Shandy*.[3]**

John Baldessari — Yes, I was approached by a publisher, and they were trying to pair up artists with books they were looking to have illustrated. The idea of illustrating a book was something I found fascinating. Two of my favorite books, which seem more like art, are *Don Quixote* and *Tristram Shandy*. The more I read about

(3) Laurence Sterne, *The Life and Opinions of Tristram Shandy*. Images by John Baldessari (San Francisco: Sterne, Arion Press, 1988 [1759-1767]).

Laurence Sterne, the more I felt I'd met my doppelganger. I think like him and vice versa. There was a nonlinear element and a tendency towards digression that felt just like me. It was a wonderful text to work with.

Hans Ulrich Obrist — **Have you done a project on *Don Quixote*?**

John Baldessari — No, but I'd still like to.

Hans Ulrich Obrist — **So it's an unrealized project?**

John Baldessari — I guess you could say that [*laughs*]. The publisher keeps on asking me to do it, and I suppose I will at some point.

Hans Ulrich Obrist — **I'm curious to hear your thoughts on Sylvia Plath and Kafka.**

John Baldessari — I was never particularly interested in Sylvia Plath; I was more impressed by the fact that everyone else seemed so interested in her. The idea of "things being under the mattress" stuck in my head. The personal habits of creative people always interest me. I remember reading about authors' habits when they write: how people sit or the paper they write with, at what time of day they write, or what they have to do to start writing and so on. I always find that fascinating because it seems like these are the same problems that artists face.

Hans Ulrich Obrist — **Kafka is also a reference in your work.**

John Baldessari — Kafka is one of my early loves—ever since my college days, in fact. His anxiety and fears—his ghosts—really motivated him. This makes him fascinating as a person, and it's mirrored in his writing.

Hans Ulrich Obrist — **Another author mentioned frequently in relation to your work is William Carlos Williams.**

John Baldessari — Yes, he has had a great influence on me, just in terms of the utter simplicity of his writing. It's the kind of quality I find in Matisse, where they look so simple but so profound. William Carlos Williams was a model for me in that he could do this with words. I've always wanted to convey the same kind of power and simplicity he achieved.

Hans Ulrich Obrist — **I interviewed Walter Hopps a few years ago and he spoke of the Duchamp exhibition he had organized in Pasadena in 1963 ["By or of Marcel Duchamp or Rrose Sélavy," Pasadena Art Museum, 1963]. It radiated throughout the whole art community in L.A. Was this of interest to you? Was Duchamp your main influence during those years? What other artists were influential for you at the beginning?**

John Baldessari — I remember Walter Hopps's exhibition. The fact that it happened in Pasadena, of all places, was something I found amazing! It took a person like Walter to do something like that. Regarding your other question, I guess Giotto [di Bondone] is my first hero in art history, and Matisse is a hero for me, too. I've never been a Picasso fan. And then came Duchamp, obviously. He was a huge influence on me, as was John Cage.

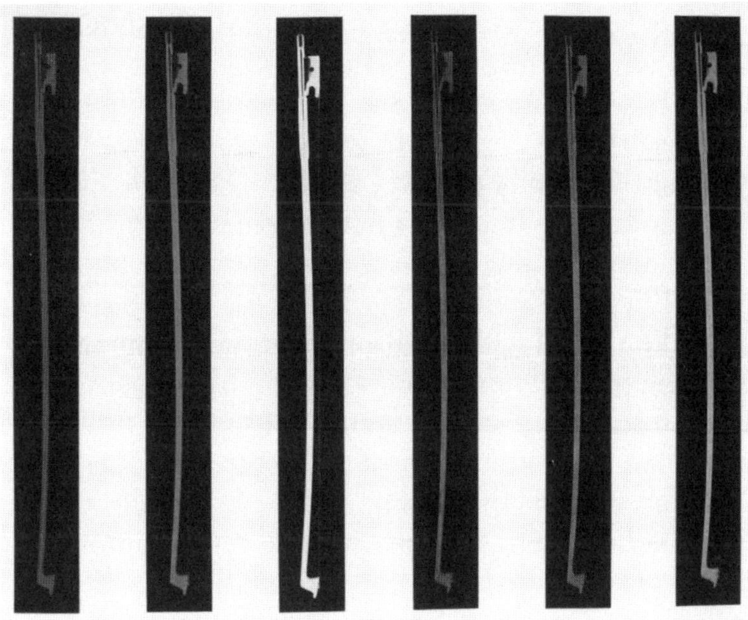

Six Ways to Pronounce Fiddlestick (for L. Sterne), 1988

Hans Ulrich Obrist — **Cage worked in the music department while you were teaching at CalArts in the seventies. Did you have an artistic dialogue with Cage while you were there?**

John Baldessari — No. I never had any dialogue with Cage, other than socially. I liked people who had connections with the art world—Morton Feldman was another person I remember. We were both in Harlem one summer, and we used to sit around and talk about art. But in terms of music, in general, while I was at the University of California, San Diego, it was an incredible department. Talking to musicians influenced me a lot, at the moment when I began to conceive of my work as existing in time. That got me into working with video and film, and it spurred me to use photographs in a consecutive way. There was this idea that if art didn't deal with duration and time in some way, it wasn't properly marrying with life. Life is about motion and time—it isn't static. This idea of time and, even in a static work, of developing the idea of time through the movement of the eye, of following a path like a road map: it takes a certain amount of time to traverse the surface. That's had a profound influence on me. Ravi Shankar was also teaching at CalArts at the time and listening to concerts of Indian music, where there is no real beginning, and no high points or crescendos. That interested me a lot, too, because it gives you another way of understanding the world—not with building blocks, but just some sort of flow. I guess my overarching concern was that I was trying to understand what art meant for me, and a lot of my early work was trying to figure out what art is and what it isn't, which can drive you crazy of course.

It was about examining all of the conventional wisdom that was around, and confronting the attitude that "you can't do that, because it wouldn't fit into art history."

Hans Ulrich Obrist — **I know that reading George Kubler's *The Shape of Time* was important to you.[4] I'm curious to know what exactly resonated for you in Kubler's time-based art history.**

John Baldessari — The two books that influenced me a lot at the time were this one by Kubler and also Thomas Kuhn's *The Structure of Scientific Revolutions*.[5] This idea of how one is located in history and time was fascinating. It's a long time ago and I can't give you exact quotes, but I do remember making a piece about how every work of art is obviously in a continuum, expanding on what came before it. It might sound like a stupid idea, but it's actually very important: art proceeds out of art. It doesn't arise spontaneously like the birth of Venus. Art arises from other art. The job of the artist, if he's any good, is to hide his tracks so you can't discover the sources. It's not a repetition of what somebody else has done before; rather, you build upon and enlarge it. You can only expect some other good artist to do the same with your work—to expand on it and not to replicate it.

Hans Ulrich Obrist — **Who are your favorite filmmakers?**

John Baldessari — I have favorite filmmakers of course, but I have to admit that I watch a lot of really bad films, as you can see over here. I'm only interested in them for the imagery. This being said, I like film noir a lot. Just

(4) George Kubler, *The Shape of Time: Remarks on the History of Things* (New Haven: Yale UP, 1962).
(5) Thomas Kuhn, *The Structure of Scientific Revolutions* (Chicago: Univ. of Chicago Press, 1962).

last night I saw a film by Anthony Mann. I like how they use light and dark. Hitchcock has always been a favorite of mine. Two of my favorite recent films are Almodovar's *Doctor* [Hable con ella, 2002]—a fantastic film—and Todd Haynes' *Far from Heaven* [2002], in the style of a Douglas Sirk film.

Hans Ulrich Obrist — **I'd like to switch gears and ask you about *National City,* which you commissioned sign painters to do. I was wondering if this was somehow related to the idea of using commercial artists or if there was a de-mystification of authorship involved?**

John Baldessari — Both, I think. Those early years were devoted to trying to figure out what art was, and authorship was certainly an important aspect. I've always been amused that painters sign their paintings. After all, it seems that with a certain amount of connoisseurship you can tell who did the painting without it being signed. More and more it's dawned on me why. It seems to be a certain basic assumption about art—that a given piece is done by a particular artist. But thinking about it, a musician does not have to perform the music he or she writes, nor does an architect have to build a house, so why should an artist have to do the work—why can't he just conceive of it? That was fundamental, of course, to conceptual and minimal art. Don Judd didn't necessary make his things. But regarding to the sign painter, the interesting thing about it was one of the things I taught myself back then, namely pen lettering and brush lettering. I don't know why I used to hang out in sign-writing and printing shops. For some reason I was very much into doing that, and I taught lettering classes for a while, so I could have painted these things myself. But I asked myself, "Why should I?" The other thing was that I wanted to use a commercial sign painter because I didn't want to have any evidence of art there. I said, "Don't try to make beautiful calligraphy or lettering—do it like a 'For Rent' or 'No Trespassing' sign. I just want information here." I didn't want it to be seen as decorative in any way.

Hans Ulrich Obrist — **How important were the emerging technologies and cybernetic thinkers for you in the sixties?**

John Baldessari — I was certainly aware of them. I was at CalArts at the time, and there we had this whole idea that TV was going to change everything. Nam June Paik was also teaching there at the time.

Hans Ulrich Obrist — **Which other artists were teaching at CalArts during those years?**

John Baldessari — In addition to Nam June, there was Allan Kaprow and Dick Higgins, Alison Knowles and Emmett Williams. Nam June was very interested in technology, and when I would drop by, I was always amazed to see what he was working on. I was interested in video, too, but I saw it just as a tool that could help me do what I wanted to do. I wasn't into technology for its own sake, nor am I into it now. I know there have been a couple of exhibitions recently in the U.S.—"BitStreams" at the Whitney [2001] and "010101: Art in Technological Times" at the San Francisco Museum of Modern Art [2001]—and I went

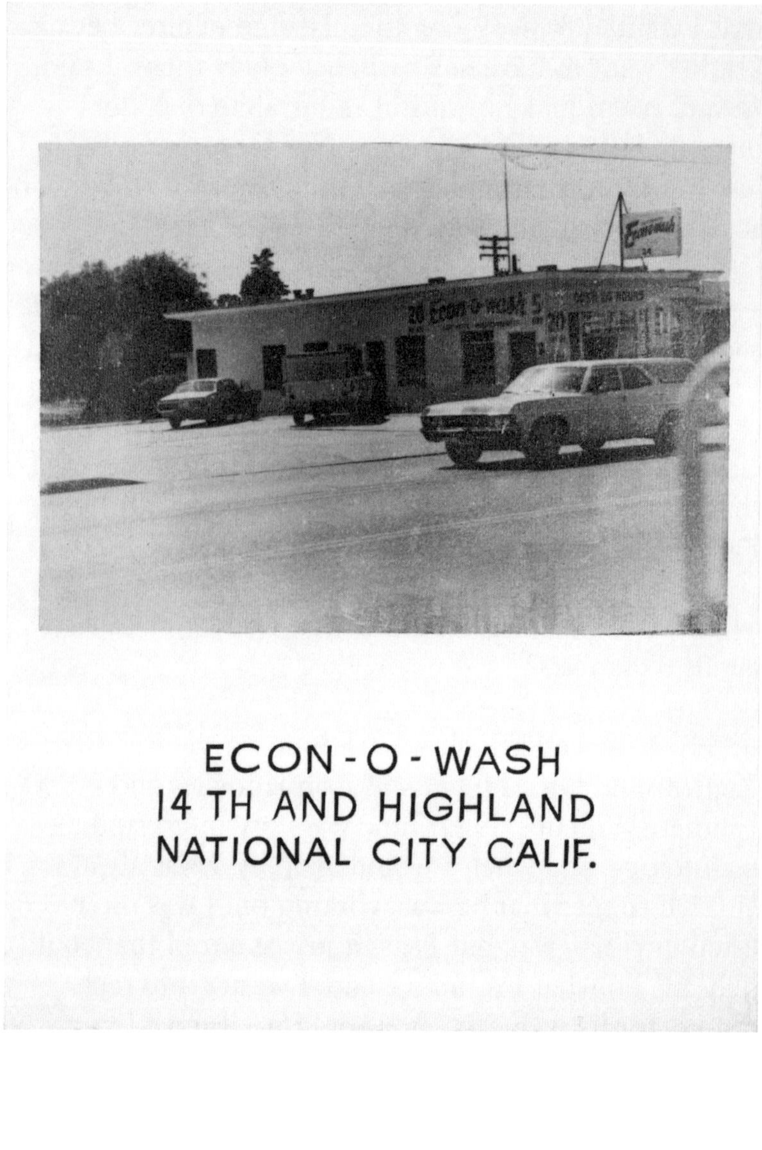

Econ-O-Wash, 14th and Highland, National City, Calif., 1966–68

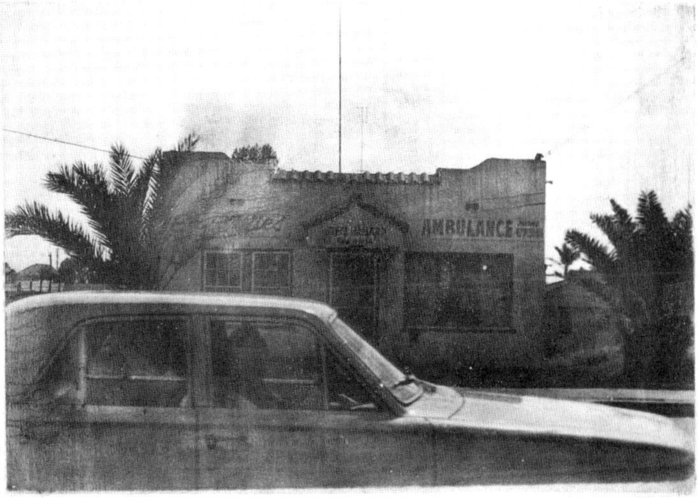

BALLARD'S AMBULANCE SERVICE
NATIONAL CITY, CALIF.

Ballard's Ambulance Service, National City, Calif., 1966–68

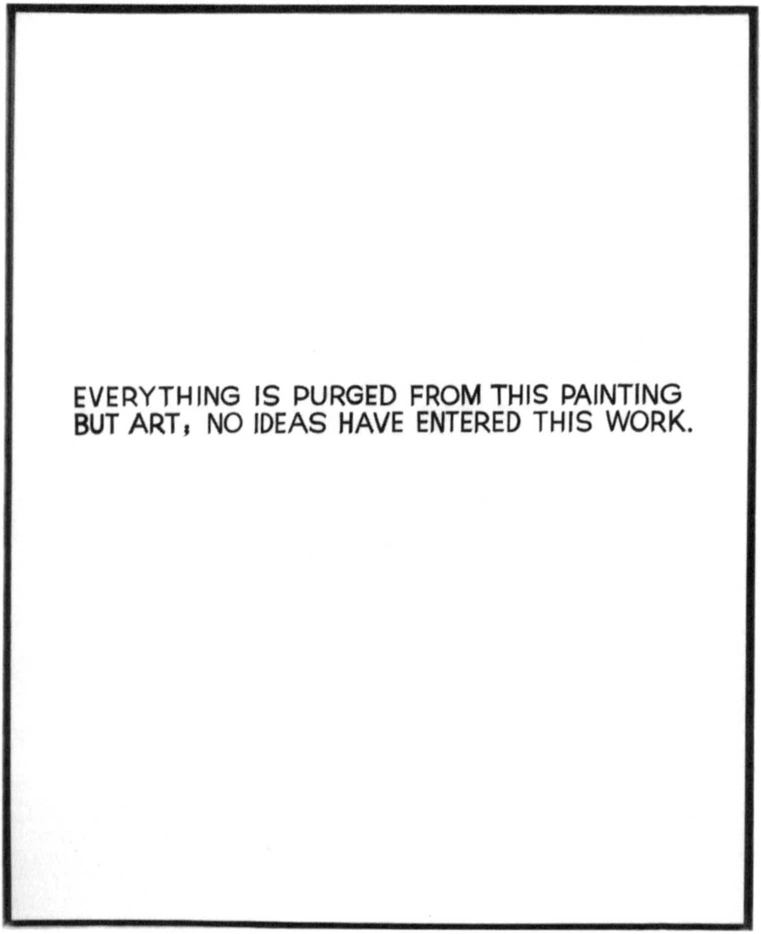

Everything is Purged... 1966–68

to both. I haven't seen a lot yet that's interested me. I usually end up just looking at what kind of screens they have or what kind of equipment they're using. And if I'm doing that, then it's probably not powerful enough. I actually did do something for MOCA that got the Art Critics Award this year for the best internet piece.

Hans Ulrich Obrist — Can you tell me more about it?

John Baldessari — Yes, it's called "Still Life: Choosing and Arranging" [Museum of Contemporary Art, Los Angeles, Digital Gallery, 2001]. It's very simple: there are two shelves, and there's an endless parade of different kinds of objects screened on the bottom one.

Hans Ulrich Obrist — Is it similar to *Inventory* [black-and-white video, sound, 23:50 min., 1972]?

John Baldessari — Yes, very much like that. It probably came out of that. And then you can choose certain things and put them on the top shelf. Not only can you put them there, but you can arrange your own sort of still life. It probably comes out of those early pieces like *Inventory* and the *Choosing* pieces [1972–73] I did. That's one of the fundamental concepts for me about art: you choose one thing over another. That's the bottom line.

Hans Ulrich Obrist — And how is your archive organized? I interviewed Gilbert and George about their archive, and almost every aspect of it is categorized—everything is neatly arranged in boxes. What about yours and the tremendous number of sources for your images?

John Baldessari — That's interesting because it grew out of my being interested in found photography and, even more specifically, in photography that doesn't look like art. I would try all kinds of devices, like way back in those pieces for *National City* in the sixties where I would just go around outside with the camera, not even looking though the viewfinder. Actually, about a year ago a former student of mind reminded me about something I'd said to him that had influenced him a lot: "The worst thing that ever happened to photography was the viewfinder." I would do all kinds of things, like setting up my camera in front of the TV screen and having it take a picture every five or ten minutes. It was never an aesthetic decision. Or I would set up a video camera outside and just photograph things automatically. Although I never did it, I wanted to put a harness with a camera on a dog and just let it wander around and take pictures. You know, in the First World War they had pigeons with cameras. I would have liked to have done that, too, or to have used a kite. Anyway, you get the idea.

A friend of mine worked in San Diego with the police department. He had a catalogue of police photography, as well as photographs of houses taken by real estate companies, or photos of accidents or cars or anything that was not meant to be art. I would go to dumps to look for photographs that had been thrown away, and I found this place that sold uncatalogued stills from movies. That's how I started collecting movie photographs. People thought I did it because of my interest in movies, but that wasn't it at all. The point was that I could get these pictures for ten cents

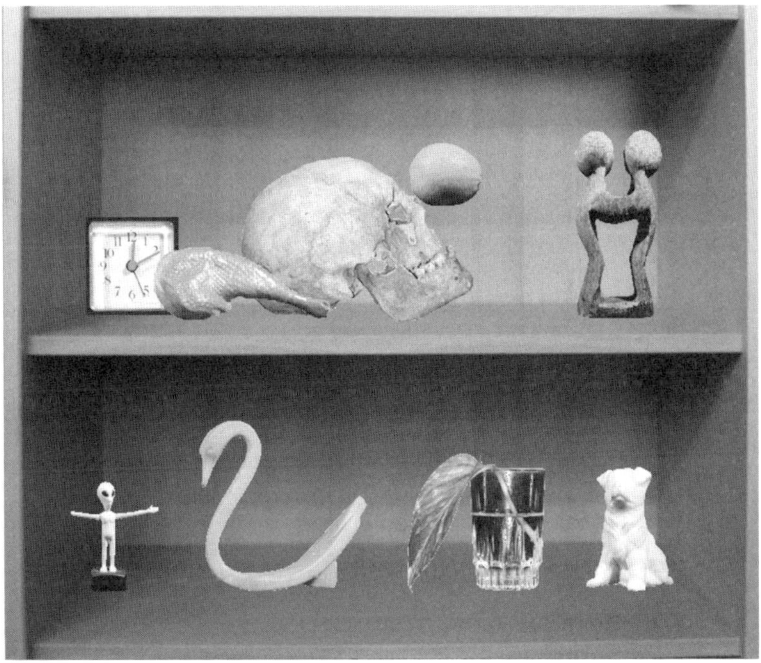

Still Life: Choosing and Arranging, 2001

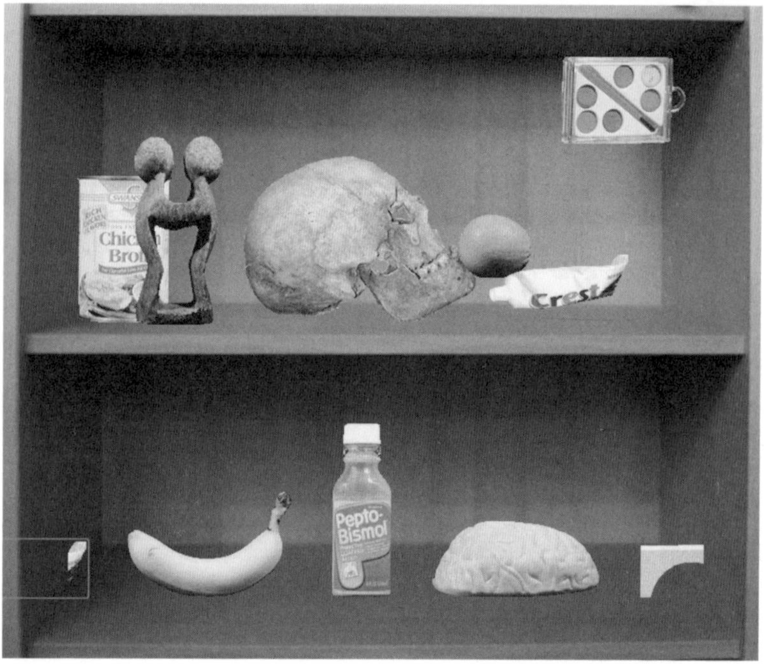

Still Life: Choosing and Arranging, 2001

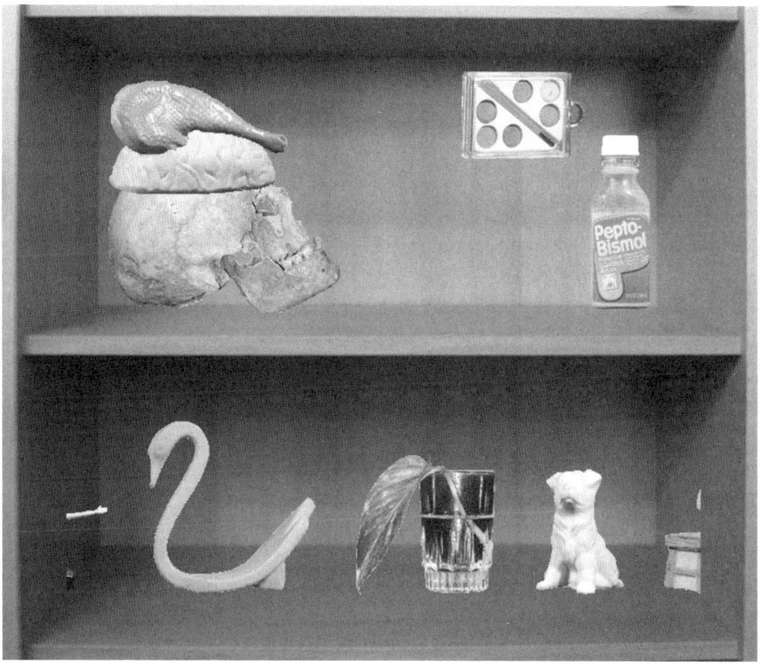
Pepto-
Bismol

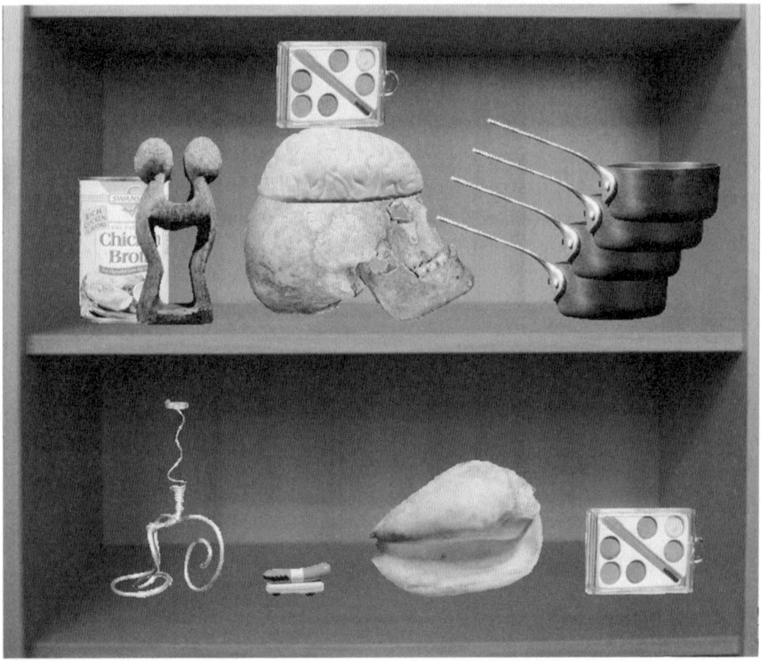

Still Life: Choosing and Arranging, 2001

each and they were mixed in with a lot of newspaper photographs. So if I had a free day I would go out there and rummage through huge bins of photographs until my eyes hurt, with the idea that somehow these might be material I could use. Then I began cataloguing them, and that's where I got into trouble. The first big category was violence: people with guns, all kinds of guns, gangster movies, war movies, and so on. Then a lot of people kissing—that's a staple for movies. Another genre is the Western. I had people riding on horses, people falling off of horses, people being shot on horses, people with arrows stuck in them on horses. But then I encountered the problem that many photographs were about more than one thing, so they became nomadic, migrating from one file to another. Eventually I realized that the files didn't help very much, so now I just keep track of them in my mind. But I still love sifting through them, because I always discover something new.

Hans Ulrich Obrist — **How many photographs do you have—tens of thousands? Are they uncountable?**

John Baldessari — Oh yes.

Hans Ulrich Obrist — **I'd like to talk about your project with Rem Koolhaas. A great deal has been written and said about your relationship to film, cinema, and literature, but not about your relationship to architecture.**

John Baldessari — I've never been overly involved with architecture, at least not in any obsessive way. I just have a layperson's knowledge. But there are architects, just like I said about musicians, who've had an interest in artists: Frank Gehry is one, and Rem Koolhaas is another. So when I was presented with the opportunity to collaborate with Koolhaas on a project proposal, I took it immediately because the idea of working with an architect who thinks like an artist seemed really interesting. And that's exactly how it turned out. Rem is beyond an architect. He's—I don't know what you'd call him—a polymath in some way. He can absorb an enormous amount of information, synthesize it, and bring it to bear on a subject. He's an amazingly open person, and it was a pleasure to bounce ideas off him and respond. At first I started out rather timidly, but then I could tell by watching his face, the way he'd respond, that the more extreme ideas were the ones he liked. I said to myself, "This guy is fantastic!"—I didn't know architects thought like this. The proposal was for a main office building for the California Department of Transportation. He was invited into the competition, and part of the commission was to involve an artist. He asked if I would work with him. It wasn't a situation where the architect does the building and then the artist comes in and decorates it with art; we actually worked together. It was a real dialogue, and I enjoyed it a lot. When he made a presentation, I remember what he said: he was responsible for the verticals and I was responsible for the horizontals. It was nice that he gave me so much credit, and it's a shame the proposal was not selected. I'd love to work on another project with him.

Hans Ulrich Obrist — **Since we're here in your studio, I was wondering if you could tell me a little about this place. You've worked** here since 1970, and your studio has become an amazingly layered kind of archive.

John Baldessari — Well, I was teaching at the University of California in San Diego from ’68 to ’70, and then when CalArts started in 1970 the chairman of the department at UCSD, who became chairman of CalArts, asked me if I would join him and teach at the new school. So I moved up here and was just working out of my house. At the time, the studio I have today belonged to another artist, William Wegman. We were both showing at the Sonnabend Gallery in New York. Ileana had a loft available and she said that either of us could use it if we decided to come to New York. I was married, and my wife didn’t want to take the children to New York, so Bill took it and asked me if I wanted the studio. I think it’s kind of hilarious now, but at the time I was working in a tiny little room in my house and I said, “Bill, it’s just too much space for me.” He suggested that I divide it up and rent it to another artist, but I didn’t and I just started out in one corner working. I think it was that corner over there. But slowly I just claimed more and more space. Now, of course, it’s too small for me. Conceptual artists aren’t supposed to need space!

Hans Ulrich Obrist — It’s a nice paradox. Regarding the art scene here, I’ve always thought that you were very close to the artists who were living here at the time, such as Bill Wegman, Bas Jan Ader, Ger van Elk, and Allen Ruppersberg. You didn’t really form a group, but conversations were taking place between all of you.

John Baldessari — Yes, we'd show each other our work because back then, with these ideas that now seem so common, you felt you were really crazy. It was like exposing yourself naked if you went to just anybody, but if you showed your work to someone who was thinking along the same lines, you gained a bit more courage. There are certain artists I was comfortable talking with like those in Los Angeles. Actually, I never really got to know Ed Ruscha very well until later, but it informed much of my approach to teaching. I would invite all the artists I liked to come to CalArts, including people like—it's such a long list!—[Vito] Acconci, Art and Language, Dan Graham, Daniel Buren, [Lawrence] Weiner, [Joseph] Kosuth. The list goes on and on and on.

Hans Ulrich Obrist — **Can you tell me more about this teaching situation? On the one hand, it involves a peer group of artists from your generation. And yet, on the other hand, you've always maintained a trans-generational commitment. For example, Liam Gillick has told me about the very important conversations he's had with you.**

John Baldessari — When I was at CalArts, the thing that motivated me so much was that I really wanted to change art in Los Angeles. Of course, this idea seems outrageous today. Most of the art here, most of the people here, were working with plastic—mostly sculpture. And I thought, "Gosh, there's all sorts of exciting art being done in the world and nobody knows about it here in Los Angeles." So I made it my mission to invite all the artists who were interesting for me to come to CalArts. It was selfish, you know—they were people I could talk to and that was the main reason, of course. There was a payoff in that the students got to talk with them, and this was largely the reason why a lot of the students became successful so quickly, because they got this information faster than any other art students, and before it came out in art magazines.

Hans Ulrich Obrist — **Can you tell me more about your teaching methods?**

John Baldessari — Well, I probably would never have started teaching at all if my sister hadn't suggested that I might need to support myself. So I started teaching in public schools and museum schools and places like that. My father and mother were both immigrants. My mother was from the middle class, but my father was a peasant. He barely knew English, so a lot of my impetus in teaching came from trying to explain things to him—to make things clear. Another impetus came from me: I felt so many things were done wrong in my art education, and I wanted to correct them. I was very excited about art—about what it could be rather than what it was. So I think my teaching method was not to say, "Do this, do that; this is bad, this is good." I took a more oblique approach, suggesting things in a way that made students think things were purely their ideas. This came out of reading somewhere that you haven't taught anything until you see that special fire in the students' eyes. For me, teaching is an art, which sometimes confuses me, because what I think I teach and what I think I do are similar.

Hans Ulrich Obrist — **And what role do the magazines play? In another interview you mentioned that you had actually subscribed to every single European art magazine you could get your hands on. It was related to the idea of getting information second hand. Could you tell me more about this?**

John Baldessari — I was born in a small city—you can't even call it a city—south of San Diego in California. It was really a ghetto, and the school I went to wasn't good at all—it was basically the kind of school you go to when you live in a deprived, low-income community. When I went to college, it was just a local college. I didn't even know who Picasso or Matisse were. I didn't know anything about art history, in fact, so a lot of what I ultimately learned was through self-education. I spent countless hours in the library just absorbing things, and when I read about this journal or that magazine I would subscribe to it, just trying to find information on my own.

Hans Ulrich Obrist — **When you were in Berkeley in 1954, you said you wanted to be an art critic. When and why did you decide to become an artist?**

John Baldessari — After getting my undergraduate degree came the inevitable "now what?" At the time, the idea of being an artist was something akin to wanting to be an exotic flower. If I had told my friends I was going to be an artist, they would have looked at me strangely and wouldn't have known what to make of it. But I was interested in art and thought, "Well, academia is respectable, so I'll be an art historian or an art critic." So I went to Berkeley to do graduate work in art history, thinking that I would get a graduate degree and end up teaching. The idea of writing art criticism interested me because I realized I had some verbal skills and liked to read and could do that. But talking to my fellow art history students, they always thought I was crazy. I remember one fellow student saying, "If I could choose between being an art historian or an artist, I'd be an artist." And he asked, "Why would you want to write about art?" That got me thinking. Maybe if I'd been in a different place where there was more interest in contemporary art I would have stayed on, but I remember the exact night I decided to quit. It was three o'clock in the morning and I was memorizing Roman coins and I said, "I don't want to do this"—and I quit. So I flew back down to San Diego and kept on painting. However, I never thought I'd be a professional artist; I always thought I'd teach and paint. But then my life changed.

Hans Ulrich Obrist — **One question I haven't asked yet is about museums. What are your favorite museums, and what do you think of the museum as an institution in general?**

John Baldessari — I'm very much opposed to official structures. A case in point is something we see in contemporary art here in L.A. The Museum of Contemporary Art commissioned [Arata] Isozaki to do their Grand Avenue facility. For the interim, they asked Frank Gehry to turn a former police car garage into a temporary exhibition space, the Temporary Contemporary. It ended up becoming so popular that they made it permanent. In fact, most artists have wanted their shows there rather than in Isozaki's building. The majority of artists I know want a space that's open, seems friendly, doesn't look official, and where you don't have to worry that you're going to destroy the place. It needs to be malleable, like a laboratory. Museums should be artist-friendly, but most of them aren't—it's more about the architecture.

Hans Ulrich Obrist — **What do you consider artist-friendly in this context? What's your favorite museum?**

John Baldessari — Well, I like the Temporary Contemporary space, I must say. I thought the Hamburger Bahnhof space in Berlin was interesting before it was started, but now it's changed. I always remember that Italian critic who did a show in a parking structure in Rome. I also like the idea of exhibiting outside major cities. Some years back I was doing shows in the same cities over and over again: Milan, Paris, London, Brussels, and so on. I said to myself that when offers come to do shows in other places, I'm going to take them. So now I've shown in places like Oslo and Reykjavík. You meet interesting people, and it's actually more challenging and fun than these time-honored places in the major exhibition cities.

Hans Ulrich Obrist — **As you know, my interviews often hide another interview, like a Russian matryoshka doll, so I contacted Liam Gillick to ask him to send a few questions for you. Here's the first one: "There seems to be a rolling sequence of recurring reference points, techniques, and images in your work. These complicate ideas of straightforward progress and more reassuring notions of producing things under a protective structure of ideas. Is this a conscious play with authorship and time?"**

John Baldessari — Wow! Well, one thing is that I've always tried to think of my works as presenting a paradox in that they look deceptively simple but are actually very complicated. Earlier I mentioned Matisse or Giotto as models. One could think of it as a detective novel—you think you know who the murderer is, but then it turns out you don't know who it is at all. You keep on running into blind alleys and cul-de-sacs; it's an infinite maze, and you get trapped in it.

Hans Ulrich Obrist — Here's Liam's second question: "How much do you edit out of a set of ideas? In other words, do we see most of the production or do some things just sit around and never get seen?"

John Baldessari — Earlier I mentioned Nam June Paik and teaching colleagues at CalArts. He made a very insightful comment once, and one that made a lot of sense to me: he said that what interested him in my work was not what I had put in the work but what I had left out of it. I realized that this is fundamental to what I do. I have an earlier piece called *What to Put In, What to Leave Out* [Super 8, color, 3 min., 1968]. It's about deprivation—about not giving you what you want and forcing you to think about what's actually there.

Hans Ulrich Obrist — Question three: "Are there any parallels between the current U.S. position and earlier moments of U.S. adventurism?"

John Baldessari — I'm going to have to give that one some thought and get back to you.

Hans Ulrich Obrist — Question four: "If it takes three men two days to plough a field with one broken stick, how long will it take one man to plough ten fields with two broken sticks?"

John Baldessari — [*laughs*] I'm going to defer on that one, too, and come up with a good answer!

II — Writing
A Conversation with Meg Cranston[6]
Studio John Baldessari, Santa Monica, California
Spring 2005

John Baldessari — "From the moment I picked your book up until I laid it down I was convulsed with laughter. Someday I intend reading it."

Hans Ulrich Obrist — **Is that a quote? That's a good beginning.**

John Baldessari — Yes, it's from Groucho Marx. He said it after receiving a book from a fellow comedian.

Hans Ulrich Obrist — **What will the chronology be? It's always great to include a very early text written about one's work.**

John Baldessari — One of my students recently put an old catalogue in my face and said, "You should read this."

(6) This conversation was conducted by artist Meg Cranston, Hans Ulrich Obrist, and John Baldessari as a discussion of a book project with John Baldessari's collected writings which will be edited by Meg Cranston & Hans Ulrich Obrist.

It was my first retrospective at the New Museum in New York City, and there was a text by Robert Pincus-Witten ["John Baldessari: Work 1966–1980," the New Museum of Contemporary Art, New York, 1981].[7] It's not bad.

Hans Ulrich Obrist — **When was it published? It would still be good to find out what the earliest text about your work is.**

John Baldessari — Here's a bibliography; it's really well researched. Let's see… interviews—it starts here.

Hans Ulrich Obrist — **Ah, so the first published text is called "TV Like" from 1974; these are the Future of Television pieces.[8] There are also pieces from much earlier, from the sixties. Clearly, the question is how far back we should go. There are notes from the mid-sixties, but we could go back even further. Is there anything from your student days? At any rate, doing this means that you win ten years for the chronology—it's fifty years of writing instead of thirty-five or forty. With Louise Bourgeois, we had a letter she wrote to Duchamp when she was still almost a teenager.**

John Baldessari — Nothing jumps to mind, but I'll make some notes here.

Hans Ulrich Obrist — **Another thing we could include is a section with texts on other artists. There's obviously the text on your own work, Meg, and texts on John's work, and then there are all kinds of different layers of texts that artists would write about other artists.**

(7) John Baldessari, *John Baldessari – with essays by Marcia Tucker and Robert Pincus-Witten and an interview by Nancy Drew* (New York: The New Museum, 1981)
(8) Douglas Davis and Allison Simmons, eds., *The New Television: A Public/Private Art – Essays, Statements, and Videotapes Based on "Open Circuits: An International Conference on the Future of Television"* (Cambridge, Mass.: MIT Press, 1977).

Meg Cranston — *Well, there are hundreds of letters John has written recommending other artists.*

Hans Ulrich Obrist — **Have you got any of them?**

John Baldessari — I've written hundreds, but I don't keep them.

Hans Ulrich Obrist — **Have you done any shows over the past few months? What about the one with Meg?**

John Baldessari — Oh yes. I'll show you the catalogue. Here it is. I'll get the catalogue out for you.

Meg Cranston — *Kim is looking for your correspondence with Kirk Varnedoe.*

Hans Ulrich Obrist — **What was it about? Were you discussing a concrete project?**

John Baldessari — No. I think the first contact I had with him was when I did one of those shows at MOMA where you use their collection, so the correspondence would have started there. And then I was on a panel about Jasper Johns—about what he did for the show.

Hans Ulrich Obrist — **That would go into the section on other artists.**

John Baldessari — Yes, and here we have a conversation about Warhol that was taped.

Meg Cranston — *This here is on Bruce Nauman and his sculptures.*

John Baldessari — This is very early. Somebody found this from when I was teaching in a small community college. We put on a show every year, inviting artists to display their work, and we gave a purchase price. It wasn't much—something like $2,000—and we used that to buy the work. This one year, Bruce Nauman had put in a piece and we bought it. I almost got fired. It was just this flat piece of steel, and underneath it said "Dark," but you couldn't read it because it was underneath. I had to defend it! [*laughter*] It's not bad actually.

Hans Ulrich Obrist — It's beautiful; it's a bit like a list, it reminds me of Georges Perec.

John Baldessari — I was answering questions that were in the newspaper, addressing them one by one. That's why it's in a list.

Hans Ulrich Obrist — Here they said, "It's for a small minority" or "It obliterates campus architecture." This is also great: "It's an abstract obscenity," "It's the students' money."

John Baldessari — And now it's worth about a million dollars, and they only paid $2,000 for it!

Meg Cranston — *Those abstract obscenities can really pay off!*

Hans Ulrich Obrist — So there's a text on Bruce Nauman and on Jasper Johns. Which other artists do you think you might have texts for? How about student recommendations?

John Baldessari — I have a lot of student recommendations. I don't know why this just popped into my mind. It's a piece of paper like that, on top. It's printed in blue, and it says "David Salle." He wrote a note to me that said, "John, I had a dream about you last night. David." That's all it said. I thought it was so weird. I saved it; it's here somewhere.

Hans Ulrich Obrist — Was it the only conceptual artwork David did?

Meg Cranston — *No, he did quite a few.*

John Baldessari — He came into CalArts as a painter, and then he immediately went into conceptual art. As soon as he got to New York, however, he realized that he wasn't going to sell any of that, so he started doing paintings.

Hans Ulrich Obrist — Are there any texts on other artists we haven't taken note of yet?

John Baldessari — I'll have to think about it, but I'm sure I have more. I have a whole file drawer with items like that note from David and other things artists have sent me—letters and postcards, stuff like that.

Hans Ulrich Obrist — I think it's particularly interesting when artists write about other artists. I don't think it has to be a very significant part of the book; it can be just a smaller chapter, with five or six people: Oldenburg, Nauman, Jasper Johns, and then a few younger artists.

Meg Cranston — *It would be great to do things that haven't been published.*

Hans Ulrich Obrist — **Definitely. That makes the book special. And how is your writing? Is it something that's very sporadic, or can it be described as a daily practice?**

John Baldessari — No, it's not a daily practice, except perhaps for email. But I am going to have to write a text over the weekend. Do you know Martin Hentschel?

Hans Ulrich Obrist — **Yes, I do.**

John Baldessari — He's doing an exhibition on an old painter friend of mine, and he asked me if I could write something about him.[9]

Hans Ulrich Obrist — **What's the painter's name?**

John Baldessari — Richard Allen Morris. He lives in San Diego, and he's an artist's artist of sorts. David Reed and I both knew him. David is from that area, too.

Hans Ulrich Obrist — **Is Richard still alive?**

John Baldessari — Yes, he is. Martin saw his work, and now he's going to show him at Haus Lange and Haus Esters.

Meg Cranston — *Have you ever done anything collaboratively with David Antin?*

John Baldessari — No, but he's written about me.

(9) Martin Hentschel, ed., *Richard Allen Morris: Retrospective 1958–2004* (Bielefeld: Kerber, 2004).

Meg Cranston — *He's a poet.*

Hans Ulrich Obrist — Where was that published?

John Baldessari — I'd like to get my high school art teacher, but I think she passed away: "I always knew John had talent." [*laughter*]

Hans Ulrich Obrist — There are also the texts you've written for shows you curated, like "100 Artists See God" [traveling exhibition, 2004].

John Baldessari — Meg actually wrote that. I can't take credit.

Meg Cranston — *Yes, I was ghostwriting.*

Hans Ulrich Obrist — How did that show come about? We didn't talk about it last time.

John Baldessari — Meg can tell you everything.

Meg Cranston — *John was asked by independent curators, because he was on the board, if he wanted to curate a show. He said yes, but then he didn't really want to do it alone, so he asked me since we had done some other shows together. After that, we started casting around for an idea, the first of which was to do a show based on something John got from LACMA. It was a piece of legislation, or a law, that described what art is and is not.*

John Baldessari — Can you believe that?

Hans Ulrich Obrist — Amazing.

Meg Cranston — *It's actually a statute. They described all the things that couldn't be art: globes are not art, maps are not art, audio-visual works are not art. We thought we'd do a show involving everything that wasn't art.*

John Baldessari — And then the obvious hit us!

Meg Cranston — *Right. Then the obvious hit us that it would look like every other show, so we scratched that idea and came up with "100 Artists See God." We liked the title and then decided we would build a show around it.*

John Baldessari — As soon as I heard it, I knew it was a winner.

Meg Cranston — *In fact, people are imitating it. There's another show here called "100 Artists See Satan" [Grand Central Art Gallery, Santa Ana, 2004], and yet another called "100 Artists see Bush" ["Perceptions of Our President," Koos Art Center, Long Beach, 2004].*

Hans Ulrich Obrist — **Did you define the rules of the game, or were the artists simply asked to interpret this particular topic?**

Meg Cranston — *The only rule was that the works had to be related to the concept of God. We didn't define it any more closely than that.*

John Baldessari — The first piece I thought of was one of Ed Ruscha's from a show that came and went without much fanfare; it was called *Miracle* [1977]. It was just a shaft of light coming down. I called him up right away.

Hans Ulrich Obrist — **Here it is, the piece *Miracle*.**

Meg Cranston — *Ed Ruscha's text is great.*

Hans Ulrich Obrist — He says: "I cannot think of God without thinking of shafts of light, and I can't see shafts of light without thinking of God." What other shows have you curated together?

Meg Cranston — *We did a show at apexart in New York a year ago.*

John Baldessari — You wrote the text for that, too.

Meg Cranston — *Yes, I did. It was called "An Interest in Life." The title comes from a Grace Paley short story of the same name. John and I both like the title of the Grace Paley book* Enormous Changes at the Last Minute. *She'd be a good writer for our catalogue.*

John Baldessari — True.

Hans Ulrich Obrist — We should definitely have a small section for shows the two of you have co-curated. There have been many more, I suppose.

Meg Cranston — *Yes. There was also "2001 1/2" [Loughelton Gallery, New York, March 28, 1987].*

Hans Ulrich Obrist — You did together?

Meg Cranston — *I was in it. Officially we didn't do it together, but I think I had—*

John Baldessari — A lot to do with it!

Meg Cranston — *Actually, our first collaboration was a show John curated called "T.V. Generations" for a place called LACE [Los Angeles Contemporary Exhibitions, 1985]; I edited the catalogue for it.*

John Baldessari — Right! I had forgotten about that.

Meg Cranston — *Was "T.V. Generations" your idea, John? How did you get involved?*

John Baldessari — I don't remember.

Meg Cranston — *I don't know where that catalogue is, either.*

Hans Ulrich Obrist — It would be very interesting to see.

John Baldessari — We must have it here.

Meg Cranston — *It must have been in 1984 or '85—something like that. We had to fight to get many of those people into the show, like Jim Shaw.*

Hans Ulrich Obrist — We should look at all those press releases, because I'm certain they contain short statements you made. We should gather all of that and have a section on your activities as a curator. What was the very first show you curated? Was there anything in the seventies?

John Baldessari — It was a scandal, actually! No, it would have been back with the show with Bruce Nauman and people like that.

Hans Ulrich Obrist — Were you the curator?

John Baldessari — Perhaps "instigator" would be a better word.

Hans Ulrich Obrist — Have there been other ones?

John Baldessari — No. That would have been the first one. I think the next one was an all-California exhibition. The way it was laid out, it was going to be at La Jolla Museum of Art and have three jurors: one in San Francisco, one in Los Angeles, and one in San Diego. Robert Irwin was in Los Angeles, I was in San Diego, and Peter Voulkos, a famous ceramicist, was in San Francisco. We each made our own selections and then worked together to come up with a final list. However, we made the mistake of deciding that artists needed a unanimous three votes to be included in the show. We couldn't agree on anybody! So that part of the show was gone. It was a real scandal! I think I was the most generous, and I remember fighting with Robert Irwin over an Ed Ruscha painting. I said, "Robert, come on," but he replied, "Look at the frame on it; it's really poorly made."

Hans Ulrich Obrist — In terms of the interviews and the writings, I think we have to make a basic decision on what to include. Sometimes it makes sense to mix things and sometimes it doesn't, but I have the feeling that, in terms of the quantity of the material at our disposal, it would be more coherent to do two volumes: a book of texts and a book of interviews.

John Baldessari — How many volumes does Mike Kelley have?

Meg Cranston — *Six.*

John Baldessari — We have to have one more than him; we have to have seven volumes.

Meg Cranston — *So we'll include recipes.* [laughter] *Another artist joke.*

Hans Ulrich Obrist — Actually, Buckminster Fuller did a book of kitchen recipes. It's a great book about dymaxion kitchens.

John Baldessari — Why not? I should save all my "to do" lists.

Meg Cranston — *Every one of his recipes starts out with "take a leek."*

John Baldessari — Or "take a clean dish." Both are possible!

Meg Cranston — *I like "take a leek."*

Hans Ulrich Obrist — Good title!

John Baldessari — I think I mentioned last time that I wanted to call this "More Than You Want to Know About John Baldessari."

Meg Cranston — *But John, you've sworn off curating, right? How many times have you sworn it off?*

John Baldessari — You know what she said when I was on this panel in Basel? I insisted, "Well, I know I'm not going to be in the next documenta of this," and she said, "They'll probably ask you to be on the selection team, and you'll ask me to collaborate." [*laughter*] I thought that was pretty funny. No will power!

Hans Ulrich Obrist — I moderated the panel the first night, and it ended up turning into a disagreement between Kasper König and Lisa Dennison. People spoke about it for weeks afterwards.

John Baldessari — It's often good when people disagree.

Hans Ulrich Obrist — Speaking of which, you have texts on your own work, and then you have texts on issues related to the work and writings of other artists. Something that often triggers artists to write is a moment of disagreement, leading to a letter of protest. Do you have anything like this in your archives?

John Baldessari — I do, actually. For example, I wrote a letter in *ArtForum* about Daniel Buren, which he replied to—also in *ArtForum*. We can find it, if you'd like. I'd done a show at the Wadsworth Atheneum, and for this particular event they invited me and Daniel ["John Baldessari/Matrix 32," Wadsworth Atheneum, Hartford, Connecticut, 1977]. Without telling me, they gave Daniel permission to put all his stripes on the wall and to put my works over his. I was furious. I didn't find out about it until I saw photographs of the review of the show in *ArtForum*. I was so furious that I wrote a letter to *ArtForum* complaining about it, Daniel replied, and that was it. We definitely need to include that in our catalogue.

Hans Ulrich Obrist — Are there also letters on political circumstances?

John Baldessari — No.

Hans Ulrich Obrist — How about letters to museums? Sometimes artists disagree with a group show and then write a letter to the curator or museum director. These are interesting documents, too. For example, there's this letter Robert Morris wrote to Harald Szeemann about why he, at no price, would take part in documenta 5 in 1972 because he refused to accept the curatorial attitude there. It's a really interesting document.

Meg Cranston — *You could do a whole book about Michael Asher.*

John Baldessari — That's true!

Hans Ulrich Obrist — Perhaps a letter you wrote to a museum will come to mind.

John Baldessari — I'll look. Usually my attitude about these things is that once it starts, it never stops. The person you're complaining about writes a letter back, and then you write yet another letter in response, and so on and so forth. And who really cares about it all other than the two of you?

Hans Ulrich Obrist — Have you ever written on museological issues, on how a museum should work?

John Baldessari — I don't think so. But this here is great—I don't know if I mentioned it to you. It's a fantastic television show with Donald Capra interviewing me. There's a local station here, and they decided to start a whole culture section. The first one was with Charles Bukowski, and the second one was with me. And then they stopped.

Hans Ulrich Obrist — When was this?

John Baldessari — It must have been 1970 or so. We have a copy of the tape.

Hans Ulrich Obrist — That "T.V. Generations" text would also be very interesting.

John Baldessari — I have it here—I'll find it.

Hans Ulrich Obrist — I'm also very interested in lists and this whole Georges Perec idea of an obsession with lists. In your writings, even as early as the sixties, lists are a recurrent element.

John Baldessari — Yes. I don't know what it is, exactly. I guess I just like the form.

Hans Ulrich Obrist — These are lists of—

John Baldessari — Things to do.

Hans Ulrich Obrist — And you keep them?

John Baldessari — No. I throw them away, mostly. But it's true: I like the form. I'll make a note of this.

Hans Ulrich Obrist — We could have a section in the book called "Lists," don't you think?

John Baldessari — That would be nice.

Hans Ulrich Obrist — It might also be interesting to create a list of every title you've ever used.

John Baldessari — How about the best titles?

Hans Ulrich Obrist — **How about also including a list of titles you never used?**

John Baldessari — We could use this list that I'm making now!

Meg Cranston — *He makes lists of his lists!*

Hans Ulrich Obrist — **Well, one list always hides another list.**

John Baldessari — I love these notebooks because they're perfect for lists.

Meg Cranston — *For sure, you have all the checklists for the exhibitions—at least for the exhibited works. You also used to have that card file with all the titles.*

John Baldessari — We still have it.

Hans Ulrich Obrist — **It would be great to have all the titles. But it's whatever you prefer: it could be all of them, or just the best ones.**

John Baldessari — Maybe the best ones, or a selection—something like that. A list of titles. I like that.

Meg Cranston — *I think John's strength as a writer is this aphoristic code to his writing, and I think his titles really reflect that, cramming a lot of ideas into a single phrase.*

John Baldessari — Multiple entendres—double is not enough for me!

Hans Ulrich Obrist — Do you have project descriptions for works of public art?

John Baldessari — I don't do much public art, but Meg does.

Meg Cranston — *I always liked the text of Jackson Pollock's application for the Guggenheim. Have you ever read it? It's really nice. I don't know if you've kept any of those over the years, like grant applications.*

John Baldessari — Interesting idea.

Hans Ulrich Obrist — That's very good. Have you kept any of those?

John Baldessari — I don't know. We'll have a look.

Hans Ulrich Obrist — In terms of public art, in the early to mid-nineties I was and still am interested in the idea of unrealized projects. I've asked a lot of artists about them. Even artists who don't usually do a lot of public art pieces often have a few unrealized projects accompanied by some texts, because the competition guidelines usually ask for a short project description. Unrealized projects[10] are often very interesting.

John Baldessari — I agree.

Meg Cranston — *We're dealing here with committees, so they don't choose the good pieces, but rather the ones that won't offend anyone. In my case, it's always the worst ones that have been chosen; the good ones never do.*

(10) Hans Ulrich Obrist, Guy Tortosa (eds.), *Unbuilt Roads. 107 Unrealized Projects* (Ostfildern-Ruit: Hatje Cantz, 1997).

John Baldessari — Well, in my case, there are some maquettes for projects. I guess there might also be some accompanying correspondence.

Hans Ulrich Obrist — Are there any projects that come to mind where there might be lateral correspondence?

John Baldessari — There is one, actually. I'm now working on a federal building, and they've commissioned three artists—I'm one of them—for it. It's not that it's been rejected, but all the correspondence is full of bureaucratese. Basically I've said, "Call me when you are ready."

Hans Ulrich Obrist — We obviously would only be interested in your letters.

John Baldessari — Yes, there are a few things that come to mind. Another one was a national campaign of artists' billboards. They were choosing one artist for every month of the year, and I think the billboards were supposed to be put up in principal cities in the U.S. It was funded by Philip Morris, and I was one of the chosen artists. And then, at the very last moment, somebody on the board of Philip Morris said they thought it was a stupid project, and that was it!

Hans Ulrich Obrist — Now that we have lists and are considering all these different kinds of texts, another sub-category we could include is instructions. We're currently working on this book called *Do It.*[11] There must be more instruction pieces.

(11) Hans Ulrich Obrist, ed., *Do It* (Frankfurt/Main: Revolver, 2005).

Meg Cranston — *There are instructions that were written as pieces and also instructions that you sent to galleries. There's one good story where John sent instructions to the gallery, and he explained how the frame should be done in red grease pencil. When he arrived at the show, all the frames were red!*

John Baldessari — I even sent a physical example of the frame along with it—and it was black. I got there and asked, "How does the show look?" The gallery owner said, "It looks fine, but there's one… Maybe you should come take a look at it. I'm not sure." I thought, "Oh God, what is it?" So we walked into the gallery, and all the works were in red frames! I said, "I sent instructions and a sample of the framing. How could you get it wrong?" She told me the framer had told her the same thing. But she got it wrong. She assumed the frames should be red because I made the diagram in red.

Hans Ulrich Obrist — Did it get changed?

John Baldessari — Oh yes.

Hans Ulrich Obrist — Do you have any instructions for other shows?

John Baldessari — Yes. The first one was for a very important show called "Art by Telephone"; I don't know if you came across it [Museum of Contemporary Art, Chicago, 1969; projects by artists on LP record].

Hans Ulrich Obrist — Yes, it was the predecessor of *Do It*. It was a record, wasn't it?

John Baldessari — An LP, yes. Some students stole it at CalArts. I don't have it anymore. More and more comes to mind. I remember with the *Information* show [Museum of Modern Art, New York, 1970], they refused to do one of the projects I was interested in, but there's a drawing in the catalogue.[12] I wanted to have an actual corpse. The idea was that you would view it through a peep-hole, feet-on like Montagna's dead Christ. Kynaston McShine's reply was, "John, I can't deal with it." Just one sentence!

Hans Ulrich Obrist — **Did they take the show off?**

John Baldessari — No, just the drawing in the catalogue. I was in the show, but it was my cookies made with ashes from my paintings [*The Cremation Project*, 1970]. I have that recipe.

Meg Cranston — *There are also the instructions for all the rubber stamps you made.*

John Baldessari — Oh yes, the rubber stamps, too.

Meg Cranston — *The rubber stamps say, "I Suppose So," "Read More." How did those rubber stamps come about? John used one of them for the cover of a magazine.*

Hans Ulrich Obrist — **Do you have them here?**

John Baldessari — Yes, I have all the stamps here. We should publish those, too. "Learn to Spell," "Learn to Read"—I would stamp letters every day!

(12) Kynaston L. McShine, ed., *Information* (New York: Museum of Modern Art, 1970).

Hans Ulrich Obrist — Are they from the seventies?

John Baldessari — Pretty much.

Meg Cranston — *It was on the cover of a journal—the first art magazine out of L.A. John did the cover, and it was just rubber-stamped with the phrase "I Suppose So."*

Hans Ulrich Obrist — What's the name of the magazine?

Meg Cranston — *It's the* LAICA Journal.[13]

John Baldessari — I think I got the idea from Sol LeWitt; he had a stamp that said "Bullshit." People would write him a letter, and he would stamp it and send it back.

Meg Cranston — *What about the scripts for your films?*

Hans Ulrich Obrist — That's a category in its own right. How many are there?

John Baldessari — There were two movies, but I also have material for the videos.

Hans Ulrich Obrist — So there are two realized movies and then unrealized movies?

John Baldessari — No, there are two movies that I did; they were realized. Then there are notes for videos.

Hans Ulrich Obrist — Do you send postcards?

(13) "I Suppose So," *LAICA Journal* (Los Angeles), no. 16 (Oct/Nov 1977).

John Baldessari — Yes, I love postcards.

Meg Cranston — *John sends wonderful postcards—very funny postcards.*

John Baldessari — That's how Walther König and I met, because he liked postcards, too.

Hans Ulrich Obrist — So does Kasper. Do you make the postcards yourself?

John Baldessari — No, they're just found postcards.

Hans Ulrich Obrist — We'll end up with seven volumes.

Meg Cranston — *We don't even need the recipes!*

John Baldessari — Eat your heart out, Mike!

Meg Cranston — *One more than Mike!*

John Baldessari — I'll call it "Eat your heart out, Mike!"

Hans Ulrich Obrist — The index of the book will become another volume...

John Baldessari — I've got to tell you a straight story. In the early days, I remember calling up Bruce Nauman; there was some show we were in, and I said, "Bruce, I always liked those instructions for performances—you know, two steps to the left, one step forward, and every crazy thing, put your nose on the wall." And he just started laughing and said, "I just make up these weird instructions to see if anybody will actually follow them!"

Hans Ulrich Obrist — Have you ever written a novel or started a novel?

John Baldessari — No, I haven't. But a whole other category would be catalogues where one is asked to write a paragraph or make a statement. I remember some for documenta 5 and 7. Jack Goldstein said he really liked what I had written. I can't remember what it was I wrote.

III — Art Basel Conversation
Art Guest Lounge, Miami Beach Convention Center
December 7, 2006

Hans Ulrich Obrist — It's a great pleasure and privilege to welcome John Baldessari to our *Conversation Series*. John has had an extraordinary influence on the artists of our generation, and his continuous reinvention of his work shows no signs of stopping. John, I'd like to start by asking you to talk about your ears-and-nose series, which you've expanded over the past few months and shows.

John Baldessari — Certainly. I had a retrospective a few years back in Vienna. The works actually started in the mid-sixties. One of them was a nose floating in the sky, and this idea held up for me. At the time, I had a friend who owned a billboard company. I would go through their surplus material with them, and of course I was getting chopped-up billboards, rather than whole ones. It always surprised me to see what would show up on these panels, and luckily one of them was a nose, and there was a beard, too. So I used them as the basis for a series of paintings. Over the years I've tended to block out certain features that I feel would normally provide important information—like faces, for example. This leads to the anxiety of not knowing what has been omitted.

But let's fast-forward now and start with the new series in Lisbon [Cristina Guerra Contemporary Art, 2006]. Thinking about that nose, I decided I would like to push it a little bit further. After gaining a reputation for blocking out faces, I decided I should do it differently and just show a little bit of the nose or an ear, or an ear and a nose. Thinking about art history, it seems that lips and eyeballs have been getting a lot of attention, but I haven't seen many examples of ears and noses. I suppose they just don't separate very well. I mean, floating eyeballs and lips seems to work okay, but not noses and ears, so I decided to free the nose and ear. Of course, the nose and the ear can have interesting sexual connotations, which was another reason why I decided to play with this combination. The title of the series was *Noses & Ears, Etc.*, the etcetera including elements like a domestic scene or a scene with violence.

The works exist on more than a single plane. It was getting a bit boring just having a single plane, so I began to include elements above or below the surface, creating three-dimensional readings. I also did prints that were neither photos nor paintings, but something in between. This all led to a different kind of reflectivity—the reflectivity of the painting and then the reflectivity of the photograph. It's given me a nice playing field to have fun in. I don't know when this series will be over—it may be over now—but I have two newer pieces here at the fair that are not in a rectangle or a square, but are shaped. That's where I'm at now.

Hans Ulrich Obrist — **Are these shaped canvases your newest work?**

John Baldessari — Yes, that's where my head is right now, but I have to see if I want to go on with them.

Hans Ulrich Obrist — **I'm curious about your exhibition I saw at the Deutsche Guggenheim in Berlin ["Somewhere Between Almost Right and Not Quite (With Orange)," 2005]. Could you tell me more about it?**

John Baldessari — In Berlin I pretty much followed the plan of the museum architecturally, including the columns and the windows. I had very tall works that went from the floor to the ceiling, somehow filling in for missing columns, and I had large rectangular works that served as surrogates for the windows. In those works, material was blocked out or hidden, and it was always orange that was painted. Then I began to play with going above the surface and going below the surface. This wasn't the first time I had used this device—that was in Zurich. With the saturated color and these forms above or below the surface, it seems like I was borrowing segments from past art, such as Matisse.

Hans Ulrich Obrist — **What about your up-and-coming project on Adam and Eve and Eden. Could you tell me more about that?**

John Baldessari — It's not a selection of works, but a project that deals with a space. It's entitled "Eden: Adam and Eve (with Ear and Nose) Plus Serpent" [Portikus, Frankfurt/Main, 2007]. On the far wall from floor to ceiling will be a black-and-white photograph of a missing head and shoulders, and you see two hands holding a snake—the serpent—that will require a wall, since it's a very tall space. The work will be painted on the wall, and that section of the painted profile will be the ear and the nose and will be elevated or sunk into the wall. The rest of the piece will be painted, describing hair and faces and so on. You have to think of it as something similar to the early King Kong, where the gorilla is looking up at the skyscraper's window—at the people inside being terrorized by these huge fingers outside of the window. It's not finished yet, but this is my plan.

Hans Ulrich Obrist — **Before we move on to your more recent work, I'd like to ask you about another show in London, which started with a lot of color ["Prima Facie (Fifth State)," Sprüth Magers Gallery, 2006].**

John Baldessari — The series of work we've seen about noses and ears started out with my wanting to get back to language again. As I've mentioned many times in the past, I try to give equal weight to words and image, at least when they're of equal importance to me. So the first works were diptychs—that is, on the one side you read the word and on the other you see the image.

The image is a close-up of a person's face, but one with a particular kind of facial expression. I would try to figure out what that person's expression might be—angry, happy, or sad—and then put the corresponding word on the other side. The whole series was called *Prima Facie*,[14] which is the Latin term meaning "first evidence," the idea being that you don't know what anybody is thinking just from the expression on their face. You could be looking at somebody in a restaurant who you think looks really upset, but it might just be bad pizza—who knows?

I like trying to match up a word with a facial expression. Then I have to consider which word is appropriate and find the matching acronyms and synonyms, as well as the color—and this over the whole series of five exhibitions. At the last one in London, I began to drop the expression completely and use just pure color. The words I would choose were those used to name paints, so if I were to ask you which paint would be used for "happily ever after," I don't know what you would say—but there is a paint named "happily ever after." Again, it would be a diptych format with the word on one side and the color on the other.

Hans Ulrich Obrist — There's permanent invention in your art. You're completing a broad range of exhibitions and retrospectives. I was wondering about how you view the notion of the retrospective considering the extent to which your work has evolved and changed over the decades. You've always remained committed to that 1971 performance where you said, "I will not make any more boring art." In terms of this idea of continuous

(14) John Baldessari, *Prima Facie: Marilyn's Dress, a Poem (In Four Parts)* (Cologne: Verlag der Buchhandlung Walther König, 2007).

reinvention, I'd like to know what the term retrospective means to you and if you could talk about the typology of this kind of exhibition. Obviously, I'm particularly curious about your upcoming Bonn experiment ["John Baldessari: Music," Bonner Kunstverein / Kunstmuseum Bonn, 2007].

John Baldessari — Yes, retrospectives are useful to an artist, or at least to me, in that you get a better picture of the works you've done over the course of your life. I remember reading years ago that the American artist [Robert] Motherwell rented a huge space and lined up all of his work there so he could work in this retrospective context. I remember thinking how fantastic that must be. That's one clear benefit of being an artist—you get to see how your work has evolved. You mentioned the exhibition in Bonn: it will be presented in two parts in the museum. It won't be a retrospective, but it will be chronological. Going through my work, they realized I had done a lot about music, so they decided to do something related to music. I'm also going to do an edition of six sculptures, though I find that such a scary word and prefer to call them objects. Because Beethoven was born in Bonn, I decided to deal with him. The objects are going to be quite tall, and there will be a very realistic ear on the wall. Coming out of the ear will be a replica of Beethoven's ear trumpet; there will be six of these. It will be interactive: you can have a dialogue with Beethoven and ask him whatever you like.

Hans Ulrich Obrist — Do you have any unrealized projects—projects that were too big to be realized?

John Baldessari — Actually, yes, there's a project I wanted to do where I would have a wall and every day a painter would come in and paint the wall a different color. It turned out to be too costly at the time. And then on the wall there would be a little framed black-and-white photograph of the pyramids, and this would be the idea of timelessness, with all of this business going on in the background.

Hans Ulrich Obrist — **In much of your recent work, such as your objects, you've taken a three-dimensional approach. Do you have any unrealized projects that are more architectural in nature?**

John Baldessari — There was the competition in Los Angeles for the California Department of Transportation. We've spoken about it before; it was with Rem Koolhaas. I was really sorry that it didn't happen in the end. Rem was very generous and wanted me to have equal credit. It's the kind of project I would like to try again, because certain things emerge in this kind of partnership that don't happen when you're working on your own.

Hans Ulrich Obrist — **What about Frank Gehry?**

John Baldessari — I bought two houses, and he agreed to do one of them, but this was before he became a world star. Gehry said he would do my house and we had great conversations about that and planning the space, but unfortunately it didn't happen because it was in the early nineties when the art bubble burst. I just didn't have enough money to do it, so the project got shelved. But we had great talks, and I always remember he was very direct. He said, "John, we are about the same age, so we have to get up and pee at night. You want the bathroom real close." He also said, "Basically, John, you want a place where you can get laid." [*laughter*]

Hans Ulrich Obrist — **I'd like to ask you about the shows you've been curating. One was the magnetic exhibition at the Hirshorn Museum and Sculpture Garden ["Ways of Seeing: John Baldessari Explores the Collection," Washington, D.C., 2006–07]. But what about the René Magritte show ["Magritte and Contemporary Art: The Treachery of Images," Los Angeles County Museum of Art, 2006–07]?**

John Baldessari — I was asked to design the exhibit; they had never had an artist do this before. So I said to myself that I was never going to get a chance like this again. Essentially, I collaborated with a dead artist, and because we couldn't communicate, I had to guess. In a way, it was like walking a tightrope, not intruding too much, striking a balance. Essentially what I did was to recycle an idea I was going to use in my Koolhaas collaboration. I realized that this entire exhibition space was carpeted with clouds and sky, so you're walking on the sky. And then you look up at the ceiling, which is covered with an aerial view of the L.A. freeway. So that's the major feature. There's also a big window, and they asked me if I wanted to cover it up or use it. Apparently it's usually covered up—it looks out over a boulevard in Los Angeles. I said I wanted to use it, but I don't want to see Los Angeles. I want to see New York at night. So there's a huge transparency of New

York at night. The wonderful thing about it is that it's similar to a double exposure, so you see very hazy New York and hear cars going by, but you also see palm trees. It's a composite of New York and L.A. by night and by day.

Hans Ulrich Obrist — **How has Magritte been an inspiration to you?**

John Baldessari — One of the main inspirations is his use of language and of signifier and signified. This theory by Saussure has attracted me for years, too. One of the objectives of the exhibition was to make Magritte visible again, since I felt he had been hidden in recent times—despite the fact that you can see his influences in magazines, design, and fashion. I consider myself to be an adherent of Matisse rather Picasso; I'm much more interested in color than in construction. I'm also very interested in Goya, who is a hero of mine.

Hans Ulrich Obrist — **What effect does an art fair have on an artist like you? Art Basel's director, Sam Keller, already quoted your metaphor about children walking in on their parents having sex. But what is an art fair like this one really like for you?**

John Baldessari — For me it's a love-hate relationship, and I often lie to myself. I tell myself that I'm not here for the art, but for a foundation meeting, and as long as I am here, I should look at the fair. I love looking at art, and I think the quality of art is getting better and better, which is fantastic. But I hate the social aspect of art fairs—it's just too much for me.

Hans Ulrich Obrist — **Damien Hirst once said, "You don't chase money with art; you've got to chase art with money." What's your take on this?**

John Baldessari — I was lucky, because money wasn't an issue for my generation of artists. I suppose if someone waved a whole load of bank notes at me and said, "Sell out here," it would have given me pause. After all, I don't think I'm any better than any other person. But money basically wasn't an issue. I was able to pursue what I was doing because I was obsessed with doing it—and I think at one point you have to be obsessed because it's very easy to get bogged down in a standard life with a home, wife, and kids. In that case, the only hours you had for your art are at the end of the day when you're dying of fatigue. Around the late seventies or early eighties I noticed that money had come into the picture: I remember speaking to a critic after a show who was really upset because she said she had wanted to talk about all the art, but the readers had only wanted to know about the prices. That was really the beginning. So now you have collectors waiting to buy your artwork before you've even graduated. I think the fallacy is that they're equating the art with the amount of money they pay for it, which is completely the wrong way to look at it. It's depressing to think of art being just another commodity.

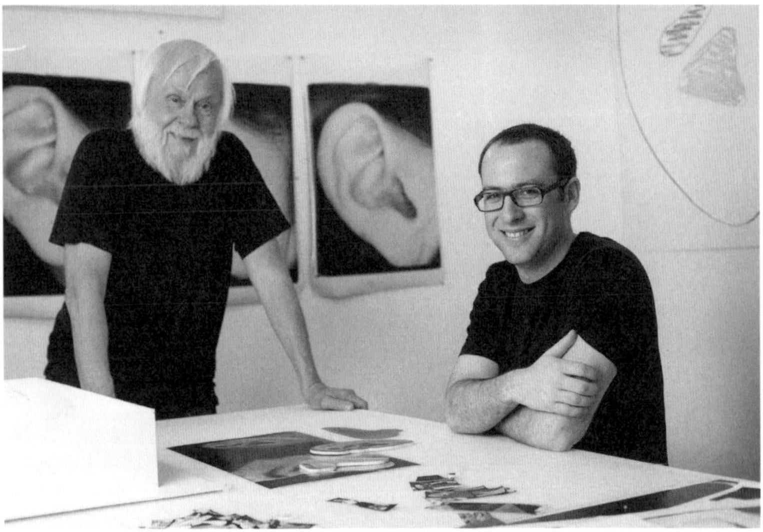

John Baldessari with Alejandro Cesarco

IV — Just an Artist with More Experience
A Conversation with Alejandro Cesarco and Rebecca Irvin
Murray Guy, New York
November 10, 2007

Rebecca Irvin — *Good afternoon, everyone! My name is Rebecca Irvin, and I'm the director of the Rolex Mentor and Protégé Arts Initiative Project in Geneva. Thank you all for being here today. I'll say just a few words of introduction and then pass over the microphone to our esteemed guests. The artists you see here, John Baldessari and Alejandro Cesarco, were brought together through the Rolex Mentor and Protégé Arts Initiative. This is a philanthropic program created by Rolex in Geneva, and it gives aspiring young artists from around the world the chance to work, one on one, with a master artist within their field over the course of one year. The program focuses on six disciplines: visual arts, music, dance, theater, literature, and film. Over the past five years, it has created a unique community of artists that spans generations and borders, and more than 200 artists and artistic leaders from forty different countries have participated. We bring each mentor and protégé together, and we set them free to collaborate in any way they choose. In the visual arts category this year, John and Alejandro have produced a work together called* Retrospective. *I'm now going to hand over the microphone to Hans Ulrich Obrist. Hans Ulrich is an international curator, and is co-director of the Serpentine Gallery in London. He was on the nominating panel that worked anonymously to propose and preselect some finalists for John's consideration, so he's familiar with Alejandro and his work.*

Hans Ulrich Obrist — Thank you very much, Rebecca. It's a great pleasure continue this conversation, which started almost two years ago in Geneva when this panel was founded. I should also mention that we had a marvelous event in London. It was a collaboration with Rebecca, Rolex, and the Serpentine Gallery, during which John Baldessari actually transformed water into wine and then back again into water. It was part of our Experiment Marathon with Olafur Eliasson in the Serpentine Pavilion. But today we're here to celebrate this exhibition—this dialogue between John Baldessari and Alejandro Cesarco. I'd like to start by asking John about the Rolex mentorship project and how the dialogue has evolved over the past two years.

John Baldessari — When Rebecca approached me about doing this, I hesitated a bit because my time was very limited. Of course, the proposition was attractive: during my many years of teaching, I've always thought it's important to provide early support and that one-on-one teaching situations are ideal—but what school can afford one teacher for each student? So when this came up I thought, "Wow! It would be great just to see what would happen." So I said yes. Should I describe the selection process?

Hans Ulrich Obrist — **Please do.**

John Baldessari — There was an international jury, which Hans Ulrich was part of. I think each member of the jury came up with four or five candidates. At their next meeting, they narrowed down the selection and created a shortlist. At that point, I interviewed the remaining candidates face to face and made my choice. And why did I choose Alejandro? Well, having taught so many students in graduate schools for so long, you know how to talk to the candidate and look at the work and get a sense of things. Sometimes, the prospective student is too fully formed, and the faculty asks, "What can we do for them? They're already out there in the world!" So you look for a candidate who's somewhere between "all over the map" and "too focused"—someone to whom the faculty feels they can offer something. What it really boils down to is an intuitive choice. It needs to feel right. I agonized a lot about it, asking myself in each case whether I could imagine working with this person for a whole year. I guess it's a bit like a relationship when you ask yourself, "Can I imagine living with this person for this long?" And when I asked myself these questions, it was Alejandro who came to mind most often. I guess I sort of had the other candidates figured out. It's a terrible thing to say, but I had a very clear picture of what they were doing and might do. But Alejandro was different: I didn't have a clue about what he might want to do. It intrigued me. He was also probably the most invisible one; his works were very evasive, very transitory, and very enigmatic. I just found them fascinating. And so that was that – it was him!

Hans Ulrich Obrist — **I'd like to know how the process of transmission worked with Alejandro. I recently reread your long conversation with one of your students, Matt Mullican, and in it you mention that you never really know when you're teaching—that perhaps the most important moment can happen while driving the car.[15] Maybe the same is also true of mentorship: the idea that it often happens in unexpected situations. Do you have a recipe for this? Did you meet regularly, or did it happen over email—how did the mentorship work in this case?**

John Baldessari — Perhaps Alejandro can answer that question best.

Alejandro Cesarco — *The year started with me spending three weeks in Los Angeles during the summer. We would hang out, visit shows together, talk about art, our likes, and our dislikes. We got to know each other's working methodologies and discussed what would be the most productive way to approach the mentoring year. John never insisted on this mentor-protégé hierarchy. Early on, he said, "I'm just an artist with more experience." I thought that was incredibly generous. So it never felt like a teaching situation in the strict sense. I'd return home and start thinking again about what we had discussed that day, and I think that was the moment where the "learning" happened.*

(15) Edelbert Köb and Peter Pakesch (ed.), "Conversation between John Baldessari, Tracey Bashkoff, and Matt Mullican," John Baldessari: *A Different Kind of Order (Arbeiten 1962-1984)* (Cologne: Verlag der Buchhandlung Walther König, 2005).

John Baldessari — I concur. I can amplify a little bit, though. It's true that I see my students as young artists who might well be better than me if they had a few more years under their belt. So I have to accord them that kind of respect. I find I listen a lot now, and I listened a lot to Alejandro. It's always a two-way street, and I'm going to learn from him as well. One thing I'm certain about is that you can't teach by lecturing, by saying this is the way to do art. That just doesn't work. But what does work? I don't know! I'm pretty sure that art can't be taught, so maybe the best approach is to have artists around who can serve as role models. You can listen to them, observe what they do, and see that they're fallible and not geniuses. You just pick up things by listening and watching. So what are the things that are being picked up? It could be anything, a chance remark. I think it's all about nourishment. Sometimes there are immediate needs, and a person needs to have a gap filled. That's a pretty easy equation. Maybe ten years down the line something I said is going to hit him and he's going to think, "Ah, that's what he was talking about!" It's about providing the right nourishment at the right time, and quite often it can be timed-release nourishment, I suppose.

Hans Ulrich Obrist — **One of the fascinating things about this collaboration is that you produced an exhibition ["Retrospective," Murray Guy Gallery, New York, 2007]. How did it start?**

John Baldessari — One of my secret goals—well, perhaps I didn't keep it all that secret—was to get Alejandro to do work that was more physical, that you could touch and feel. It was bit contrary to what he had been doing. I wondered at first whether it was really a good approach, but I wanted to see how he would pick up on it. So I began to encourage him and we came up with an idea we both thought was good and didn't violate any of our working principles. We're both very interested in language and the written word, so it was a simple two-way exchange. He initiated it and came up with a series of twelve silkscreen images that looked like pages from a book. The color choices were his, as was the first text. What I did was simply the marginal notes—maybe a reply to what he had written and my reaction to it. Quite often they're ironic. It could have gone on and on, back and forth and back and forth, but I think we're happy with the way it turned out. We decided we'd also make it into a book; it's a hybrid kind of work.[16]

Alejandro Cesarco — *Just in terms of working together, I think it was easier for us to talk about a third element, something concrete. The show is called "Retrospective" and it has to do with looking-back and marginally framing a text that is disappearing or has been partially erased or forgotten. So, in the work the narrative force is carried forward, or occurs, through footnotes. It's interesting that John assumed what he referred to as a somewhat ironic position towards the work. I think there is something quite revealing, and perhaps liberating, in assuming this ironic distance towards one's own history or how one fits or is fitted into history.*

Hans Ulrich Obrist — **Perhaps we can talk a little bit about language. While preparing this conversation, I read interviews you both gave in different contexts. You both refer to [Ferdinand]**

(16) John Baldessari and Alejandro Cesarco, *Retrospective* (Cologne: König, 2007).

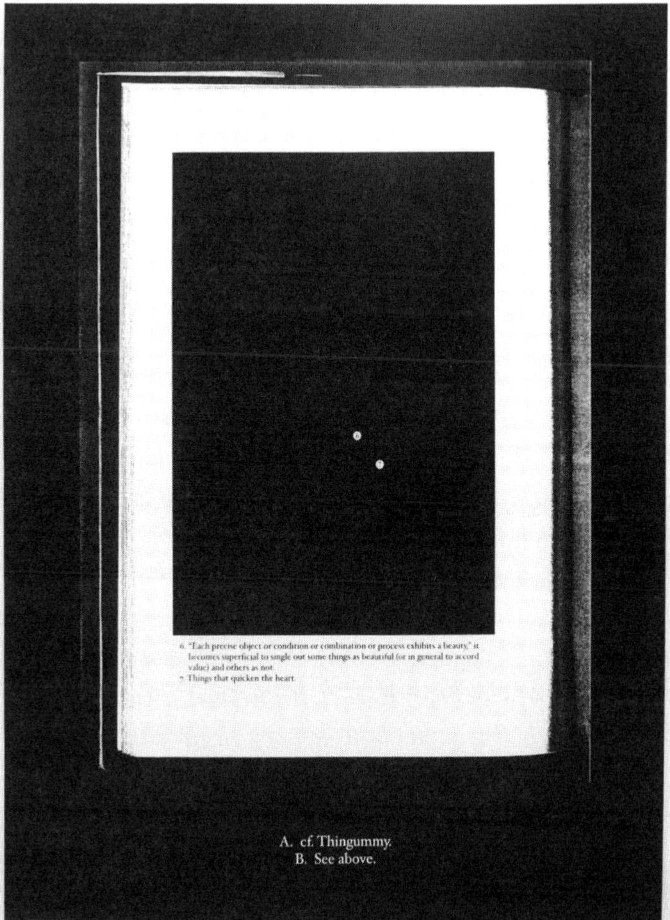

Retrospective (#9), 2007

de Saussure as a major influence. There's a passage, John, where you describe how Alejandro's language functions as a system—pre-determined or inherited, as de Saussure would say—or as a set of rules, more Chomskyan in fashion.

John Baldessari — At one point I was very much into structuralist thought and how language works. It's just a system, arbitrary in some cases, with sets of cultural rules. It was fascinating to me because that was pretty much where my own work was going anyway. So, yes, I think my early work was very much influenced by the structuralists.

Alejandro Cesarco — *I'm obviously interested in theories of language, too, but from the position of an amateur with all the insecurities that entails. It's very different to read these texts in, say, a graduate course and have someone guide you than it is to approach them on your own, when you often have to ask yourself, "Am I really understanding what this person is saying?" "Is this the 'right' reading?" This creates an interesting tension. However, I often think my work has more to do with ideas of the book than with actual theories of language. Though this is perhaps a very slight distinction.*

Hans Ulrich Obrist — You also have many other points in common: the idea of book, for example, and also the fact that you're both curating exhibitions. I'd like to talk more about the exhibition, which everyone in the audience will hopefully have time to discover after this talk. I was particularly intrigued by the title, "Retrospective," especially at a time when you, John, are working with Jessica Morgan on a major retrospective for the Tate. Could you both please elaborate a little on the title? What's the link to a retrospective?

John Baldessari — Alejandro is the one who came up with the title, so I think we should ask him.

Alejandro Cesarco — *It began with my thinking about what is implied in looking back and how one retells the past. The title addresses this dialectic between remembering and forgetting, and what kinds of differences are created in the act of re-telling. That is, what fictions are inevitably constructed in these acts of editing information, of canceling or removing facts. This is something that obviously John has been involved with in his art practice but also something that he has been subject to or participated in, in terms of the construction of art history. It also came from trying to address the age of experience gap between John and me. I was interested in how that vantage point, or how that delay, would be reflected in the works. And on a more playful note, it was also a way to somehow start in the future and look back.*

Hans Ulrich Obrist — John, how do you participate in your historization?

John Baldessari — I'm beginning to get involved in it again—for example with the retrospective coming up at the Tate in 2009. The curator doesn't want to replicate my earlier retrospectives, so that leaves me with the question of how it'll be presented. It's kind of scary. Over the years, I've always had a difficult time reading things about me because it seems like they're describing somebody else. I guess it'll always be that way; you'll always be someone else. At any rate, the show is a collaborative thing: it's the curator's show as well, and I don't want to intervene in her idea of me. Whatever these shows may be, they're a picture of you, and maybe you yourself have it wrong. It's very confusing and mysterious. One thing I really like about Jessica's approach is that she's using a lot of works that haven't seen the light of day for thirty or forty years.

Hans Ulrich Obrist — I have one last question about "Retrospective," about the show here, today. Having worked with John and Meg Cranston on a book of his collected writings, I was wondering where the texts in these works come from—whether they're found texts, or texts you wrote yourselves. There's also a very interesting moment when John doesn't answer with a text, but with a picture. I'm curious as to where the image came from.

Alejandro Cesarco — *Half of the texts were appropriated, and half were written by us. I don't feel that in this case it's very important to clarify the sources of references. It's okay if it stays unclear. The group of initial footnotes somehow articulate what we were talking about before—a narrative structure with which to look back. They also manage to place an unnamed subject within this specific framework.*

John Baldessari — Perhaps, in the process of teaching, one tries to attack what the young artists are saying in a mild way, to get to the bottom of things. Alejandro probably suffered from it a bit, too. But this may give you an idea of my comment: he produces a text, and I make these asides, these marginal notes to myself. I think marginal notes are sometimes notes to the author; you don't really get to say things face to face, but you write them down anyway.

Hans Ulrich Obrist — What about that one image?

John Baldessari — It's one of the hallmarks of my character. Why just have written comments when you can also reply with an image? I think I'm presenting a list of possibilities for characters, so it's a crowd chart—a found crowd chart.

Hans Ulrich Obrist — **Now that we've discussed the notion of the retrospective, I'd like to turn to curatorial questions. Both of you, in addition to your work as artists, have also curated shows. I'd like to know more about them.**

John Baldessari — The advantage of artists curating shows is that they see and bring out connections that other people might not see. I've also found that artists can get away with things that professional curators can't, because the curators have their peers, too. They can always say, "Well, that happened because it was an artist, and everybody knows that artists are crazy!" So I like to see art shows curated by artists. I think more artists should do that, but they don't always have the time.

Hans Ulrich Obrist — **Another important element for you, Alejandro, is literature. You've published several works and translated a book of love poems [by the Uruguayan poet Idea Vilariño].[17] Literature and dialogue with other writers have always played a very big role in your work. Could you tell us about this?**

Alejandro Cesarco — *For me, it's more a fascination with storytelling, because I'm interested not only in literature, but in film as well. Translating also fascinates me. I'm very interested in these shifts of perspective or, as John was saying,*

(17) Idea Vilariño, *Love Poems*, transl. by Alejandro Cesarco (Austin: testsite/fluent~collaborative, 2004). Originally published under the title *Poemas de amor* Montevideo: Número, 1957).

this possibility of making something invisible and figuring out how such a minor shift can make a major difference. A very Borgesian idea.

Hans Ulrich Obrist — What about your publishing house?

Alejandro Cesarco — *Well, it's a small, non-profit publisher called A.R.T. Press where I edit an ongoing series of conversation based books titled "Between Artist" that document the different positions and strategies of a number of artists. The books are open in terms of form and content in that the participating artists jointly define the concerns of each book.*

John Baldessari — I've always thought that artists, when they're doing their work, are in conversation with other artists—that they're saying something via their work. In other words, if you said something meaningful, then artists are saying something back to you with their work. That's what would interest me about these books.

Hans Ulrich Obrist — Looking at this Rolex Arts Initiative, I think we can see that it's one of these rare moments when a program really involves all disciplines and goes beyond the fear of pooling knowledge. Both of you have explored various links to literature and music. But before we move on to music, I'd like to ask John about his link to literature, because he's also collaborated with poets. I'm thinking of the dialogue with David Antin; I also see Frederic Tuten, the novelist, is here today. The relationship between art and literature has played such a key role in all the avant-gardes of the twentieth century, even if it's perhaps less present at the moment than links to other disciplines.

John Baldessari — I actually read more about writers and musicians because they have similar lives, and it's a way for me to get distance. If I read about another artist—about his working habits and so on—it's just too close. I say, "Yeah, I know that already." But if I'm reading about a writer who has the same habits I say, "Wow! You too?" It seems that all creative people have similar problems and think similar thoughts. I shared an office in the seventies with the poet David Antin, and he brought by a lot of New York poets who came to us to read. It was fantastic for me to have conversations with them. I had always read poetry and books, but had never met many of the poets. When you actually meet them and have conversations with them, it's an incredible experience. I've also been very fortunate at where I've been able to teach. UC had a fantastic music department, as did CalArts. I had great conversations with musicians, and many of them influenced me quite a bit. I've really been very lucky.

Hans Ulrich Obrist — Alejandro, you've worked with poets and writers of your own generation, but you've also rediscovered older pioneers. I'm thinking here primarily of your Idea Vilariño translation. Can you tell us more about this?

Alejandro Cesarco — *Sure. Though I wouldn't quite call it a discovery as she is very well known and recognized in Uruguay; mine is simply the first ever English translation of her book. For me, the project involves a covert form of appropriation that attempts to investigate the potential of literal translation as a visual act. Establishing an economy of means by speaking through someone else's words. Something that could be considered as an emotional ready-made. Vilariño is a poet I read throughout my teenage years, and with whom I identified and I remained fond of her work. I don't know whether I can elaborate on it much more than that.*

Hans Ulrich Obrist — **Then let's switch gears and talk about music, because that's perhaps an even more important chapter. You, John, have an exhibition in Bonn called "Music" ["John Baldessari: Music," Bonner Kunstverein / Kunstmuseum Bonn, 2007]. And you, Alejandro, make these annual play lists.**

John Baldessari — The Kunstmuseum in Bonn wanted to put on a retrospective show, but the Tate became a little worried about having another retrospective preceding theirs. So the curator in Bonn went through my archive and came up with the idea of music. He said, "You've done a lot of work with music as a theme"—and, you know, it hadn't dawned on me. The whole exhibition is chronological, showing works in which I dealt with the subject of music. And then parallel to that, the Kunstverein in Bonn, which has no collection, wanted me to do a project for them. Bonn is the birthplace of Beethoven, so I visited the Beethoven house and was very much taken with the display case of the composer's ear trumpets. Some of them were really quite beautiful. Since I had been working thematically with the subject of noses and ears in my ongoing work, this led to the epiphany. I called this guy who does sculpture editions and told him about my idea. He'd been after me for years, but I'd always told him I don't do sculpture. This time it was different, though. So there are six works—all six-foot-tall white ears taken from Michelangelo's David. Then I chose one of Beethoven's ear trumpets and made an exact reproduction, except for the fact that it's large—the bell is four feet wide. There are six of them, and they're interactive: if you speak into the bell, it will play back a snippet of one of the late quartets.

Hans Ulrich Obrist — Alejandro, can you tell us more about these lists of music you send to friends as printed matter—these play lists? I was once told that it's very important in interviews to ask artists what music they listen to while they work.

Alejandro Cesarco — *I've been sending this compilation CDs to a growing number of friends for the past seven or eight years. It has to do with a language of emotions really. All the CDs are sent along with some printed matter and the following phrase, "This is a soundtrack. You are a movie." These songs that function again almost like emotional ready-mades that accompany me throughout the year, and at the end of the year I send them—whatever I've been listening to the most—to my friends.*

Hans Ulrich Obrist — What's on the most recent list?

Alejandro Cesarco — *To be honest, this is the first year that I've skipped. I didn't make one, but I was actually thinking about it recently. I've been listening non-stop to this album by Gal Costa, called "Gal a Todo Vapor." Maybe I'll just send out the complete album.*

Hans Ulrich Obrist — Before we go over to see the exhibition, I'd like to begin the third and last chapter of the interview. I was watching *Inside the Actors Studio* the other day, and, as you know, all of the interviews end with the famous Bernard Pivot questionnaire. I thought it might be interesting to end the

conversation today in the same way. So my first question to both of you is: what's you favorite word?

John Baldessari — Word? Well, the one I've been thinking about the last week or so is "popinjay." It's an old word that you usually only see in the literature; you don't hear it very often. But I was watching the old Zorro movie again with—is it Errol Flynn? I forget. Anyway, when he's not being Zorro, he's this kind of foppish guy, and he's called a popinjay. I haven't heard that used for people in a long time. I think I'll find somebody to use it on [*laughter*].

Alejandro Cesarco — *I like the word "maybe"* [laughter].

John Baldessari — Maybe?

Alejandro Cesarco — *Maybe.*

Hans Ulrich Obrist — **What's your least favorite word?**

John Baldessari — [*laughs*] My least favorite word? I don't know. I'll pass.

Alejandro Cesarco — *I could use "maybe" again.* [laughter]

Hans Ulrich Obrist — **What turns you on creatively, spiritually, or emotionally?**

John Baldessari — Seeing good art.

Alejandro Cesarco — *I think I'll pass.*

Hans Ulrich Obrist — **And what turns you off?**

John Baldessari — What turns me off? Boredom. I get bored very easily.

Alejandro Cesarco — *Frustration.*

Hans Ulrich Obrist — **And now returning to sound: what sound or noise do you love?**

John Baldessari — Well, last night there was this beep-beep-beep in my hotel room at three o'clock in the morning.

Hans Ulrich Obrist — **You liked that?**

John Baldessari — No, I hated it!

Hans Ulrich Obrist — **And the one you love?**

John Baldessari — When you say I'm terrific, of course! [*laughter*]

Alejandro Cesarco — *I like the sound of waves. And as to what sounds turn me off… anything that I can't shut off.*

Hans Ulrich Obrist — **What profession other than your own would you like to attend?**

John Baldessari — I could be flippant here and say if you can be an artist, you can also be a brain surgeon. You can do your brain surgery on weekends as an amateur.

Alejandro Cesarco — *I don't know. I'm not sure.*

Hans Ulrich Obrist — What profession would you not like to do?

John Baldessari — I've always avoided administrative jobs.

Alejandro Cesarco — *I think I wouldn't want to be responsible for other people.*

Hans Ulrich Obrist — After a recent interview with Matthew Barney, he sent me a DVD of Al Pacino in *Inside the Actors Studio*. It's what triggered my idea to ask questions like these in my interviews. When asked the question about professions, Al Pacino said that he really wouldn't like to move furniture. The last question was, "If heaven exists, what would you like to hear God say when you arrive at the Pearly Gates?" Al Pacino answered, "Rehearsal at three" [*laughter*]. What would your answer be?

John Baldessari — Long time no see! [*laughter*]

Alejandro Cesarco — *I'll pass.*

Hans Ulrich Obrist — I'd like to ask one very last question. I was wondering, Alejandro, what you feel is the most important thing you learned from John in terms of process.

Alejandro Cesarco — *I learned to simply do things and not worry so much about foreseeing the end result. I tend to usually work in a very controlled manner, and I'm very slow. I think it ultimately has to do with self-censorship. What I learned from John was to go ahead and do things, and that it's fine if mistakes are made. There will most likely be another chance…*

Hans Ulrich Obrist — And one very last question to John: Rainer Maria Rilke wrote a wonderful little book of advice to a young artist. What would your advice be?

John Baldessari — I guess it would be that talent is cheap, but to be good you have to be obsessed.

Hans Ulrich Obrist — Many, many thanks to John Baldessari and Alejandro Cesarco!

John Baldessari

Born in 1931 in National City, California. Attended San Diego State University and did post-graduate work at Otis Art Institute and the University of California at Berkeley. He taught at the California Institute of the Arts in Valencia, CA from 1970–1988 and the University of California at Los Angeles from 1996–2007. His artwork has been featured in more than 200 solo exhibitions and in over 900 group exhibitions in the U.S. and Europe. His projects include artist books, videos, films, billboards and public works. His awards and honors include memberships in the American Academy of Arts and Letters, the Oskar Kokoschka Prize. Baldessari's recent projects include solo shows in New York, Europe, and Los Angeles; books; films; retrospectives at the Museum Moderner Kunst Stiftung Ludwig Wien in Vienna, Austria (2005), the Kunsthaus Graz in Graz, Austria (2005), and at the Carré d'Art, Musée d'Art Contemporain in Nimes, France (2005). Upcoming exhibitions include Museum Haus Lange in Krefeld, Germany, Galerie Greta Meert in Brussels, and a traveling retrospective that begins at the Tate Modern in London in 2009. John Baldessari lives and works in Santa Monica, California.

Hans Ulrich Obrist

Born in Zurich in 1968. Since 2006 he has served as Co-director of Exhibitions & Programmes and Director of International Projects at the Serpentine Gallery in London, where he currently lives and works. From 1991 to the present, he has curated 150 exhibitions in various fields of contemporary art. In addition to these projects, he is the editor of a series of artist books published by Verlag der Buchhandlung Walther König.

Thanks to
(in alphabetical order)

Herbert Abrell
Michael Amzalag &
Mathias Augustyniak
Daniel Birnbaum
Stefano Boeri
Erica Bolton
Francesco Bonami
Thomas Boutoux
Alejandro Cesarco
Meg Cranston
Maria Finders
Joachim Geil
Liam Gillick
Janice Guy
Eric Hobsbawm
Jens Hoffmann
Rebecca Irvin
Bree Jeppson
Samuel Keller
Kasper König
Walther König
Rem Koolhaas
Bettina Korek
Gunnar Kvaran
Suzanne Lacy
Karen Marta
Isabela Mora
Julia Peyton-Jones
Jane Quinn
Sally Tallant
Lorraine Two
Jonathan Wingfield

The Conversation Series.
Hans Ulrich Obrist

Already published:

The Conversation Series 1.
Robert Crumb.
Hans Ulrich Obrist.
ISBN: 978-3-88375-948-7
€ 9.80 / CHF 18.50

The Conversation Series 2.
John Chamberlain.
Hans Ulrich Obrist.
ISBN: 978-3-88375-922-7
€ 12.80 / CHF 24.–

The Conversation Series 3.
Konrad Klapheck.
Hans Ulrich Obrist.
Hans-Peter Feldmann.
ISBN: 978-3-86560-035-6
€ 12.80 / CHF 24.–

The Conversation Series 4.
Rem Koolhaas.
Hans Ulrich Obrist.
ISBN: 978-3-86560-077-6
€ 9.80 / CHF 18.50

The Conversation Series 6.
Wolfgang Tillmans.
Hans Ulrich Obrist.
ISBN: 978-3-86560-133-9
€ 14.80 / CHF 27.50

The Conversation Series 7.
Yona Friedman.
Hans Ulrich Obrist.
ISBN: 978-3-86560-171-1
€ 14.80 / CHF 27.50

The Conversation Series 8.
Zaha Hadid.
Hans Ulrich Obrist.
ISBN: 978-3-86560-078-3
€ 14.80 / CHF 27.50

The Conversation Series 9.
Gilbert & George.
Hans Ulrich Obrist.
ISBN: 978-3-86560-217-6
€ 16.80 / CHF 31.–

The Conversation Series 10.
Thomas Demand.
Hans Ulrich Obrist.
ISBN: 978-3-86560-204-6
€ 16.80 / CHF 31.–

The Conversation Series 11.
Nancy Spero.
Hans Ulrich Obrist.
ISBN: 978-3-86560-322-7
€ 14.80 / CHF 27.50

The Conversation Series 12.
Dominique Gonzalez-Foerster.
Hans Ulrich Obrist.
ISBN: 978-3-86560-334-0
€ 16.80 / CHF 31.–

The Conversation Series 13.
Olafur Eliasson.
Hans Ulrich Obrist.
ISBN: 978-3-86560-335-7
€ 16.80 / CHF 31.–

The Conversation Series 14.
Philippe Parreno.
Hans Ulrich Obrist.
ISBN: 978-3-86560-340-1
€ 16.80 / CHF 31.–

The Conversation Series 15.
Enzo Mari.
Hans Ulrich Obrist.
ISBN: 978-3-86560-401-9
€ 12.80/ CHF 24.–

The Conversation Series 16.
Gustav Metzger.
Hans Ulrich Obrist.
ISBN: 978-3-86560-498-9
€ 14.80 / CHF 27.50

The Conversation Series 19.
Christian Boltanski.
Hans Ulrich Obrist.
ISBN: 978-3-86560-513-9
€ 22.– / CHF 39.–